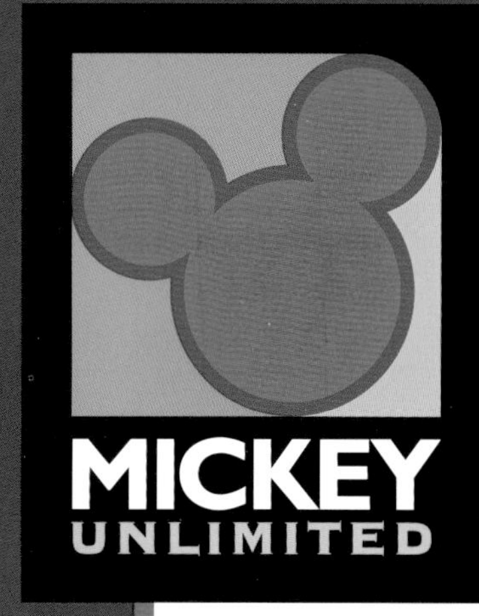

Join the Disney parade, and let Mickey and buddies give your spirits a supercharged boost with their megawatt smiles! This Mickey Unlimited Ultimate Cross Stitch Collection *features the animated antics of Disney characters on home decorations and accent pieces. You'll be charmed by the lighthearted capers of our cartoon friends — whether they're swinging to jukebox tunes, cruisin' in a vintage car, or just whistling a happy tune. You can choose from oodles of projects ranging from framed pieces and pillows to afghans and coasters and so much more! Discover the joy of displaying fun-loving designs in your home or giving them to extra-special friends. You'll find that Mickey and his pals are pros at lighting up faces with ear-to-ear grins!*

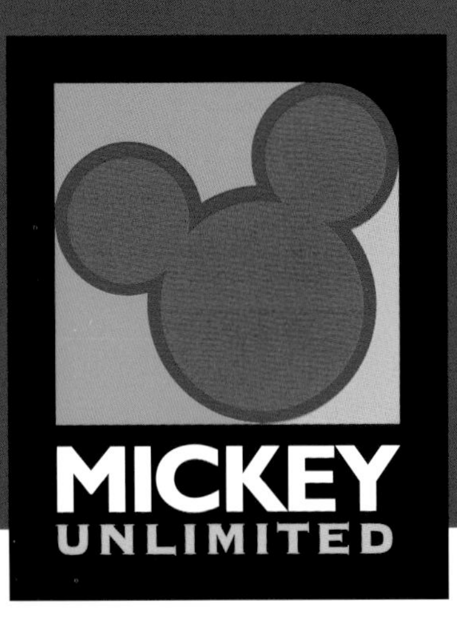

ULTIMATE CROSS STITCH COLLECTION

Library of Congress Catalog Number 98-67367
International Standard Book Number 1-57486-142-5

Table of Contents

Chart on pages 26-2

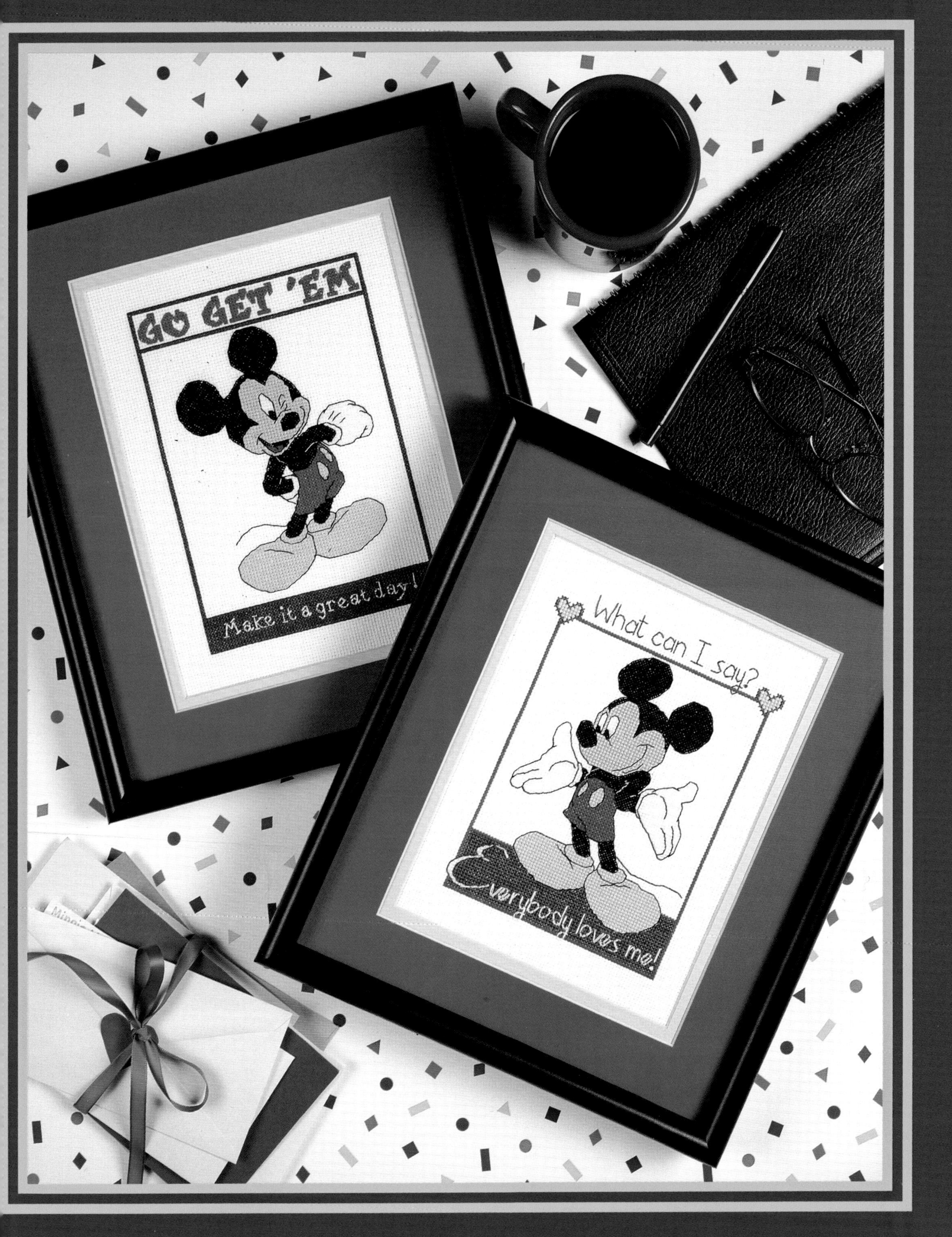

Charts on pages 28-29

Chart on pages 30-3

Charts on pages 32-33

Charts on pages 36-3

Whistle a happy tune.

Charts on page 46

...harts on pages 42-45

Charts on pages 48-

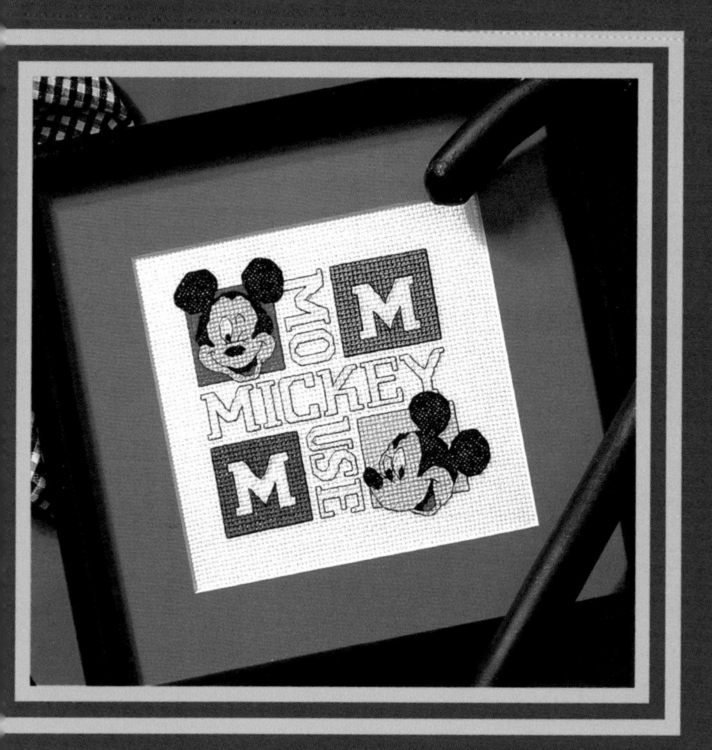

arts on pages 50-51 and 94

Chart on page

Chart on pages 52-53

Charts on pages 54-

harts on pages 54-56

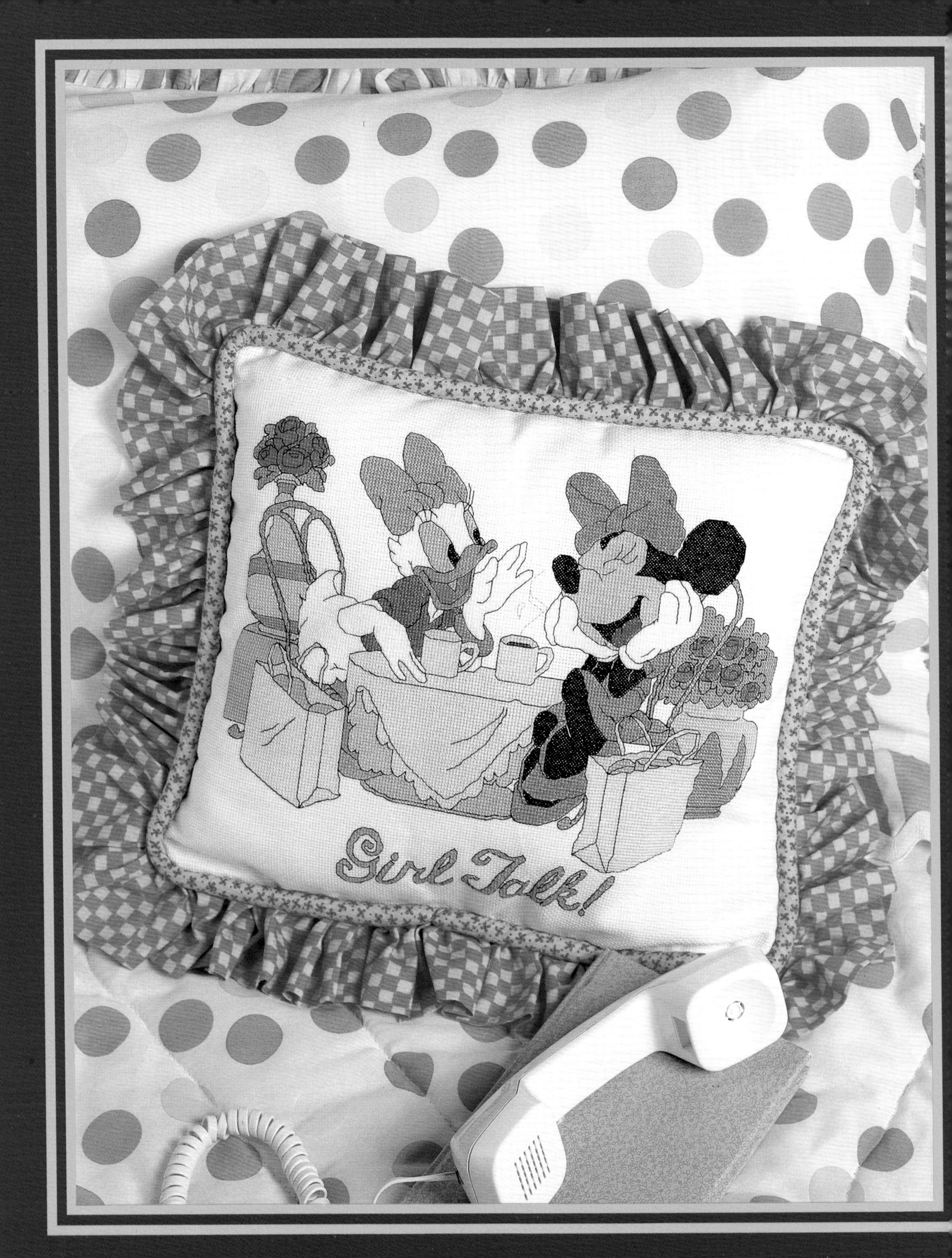

Chart on pages 62-

Charts on pages 58-61

Charts on pages 66-7

Charts on pages 54-55 and 72-73

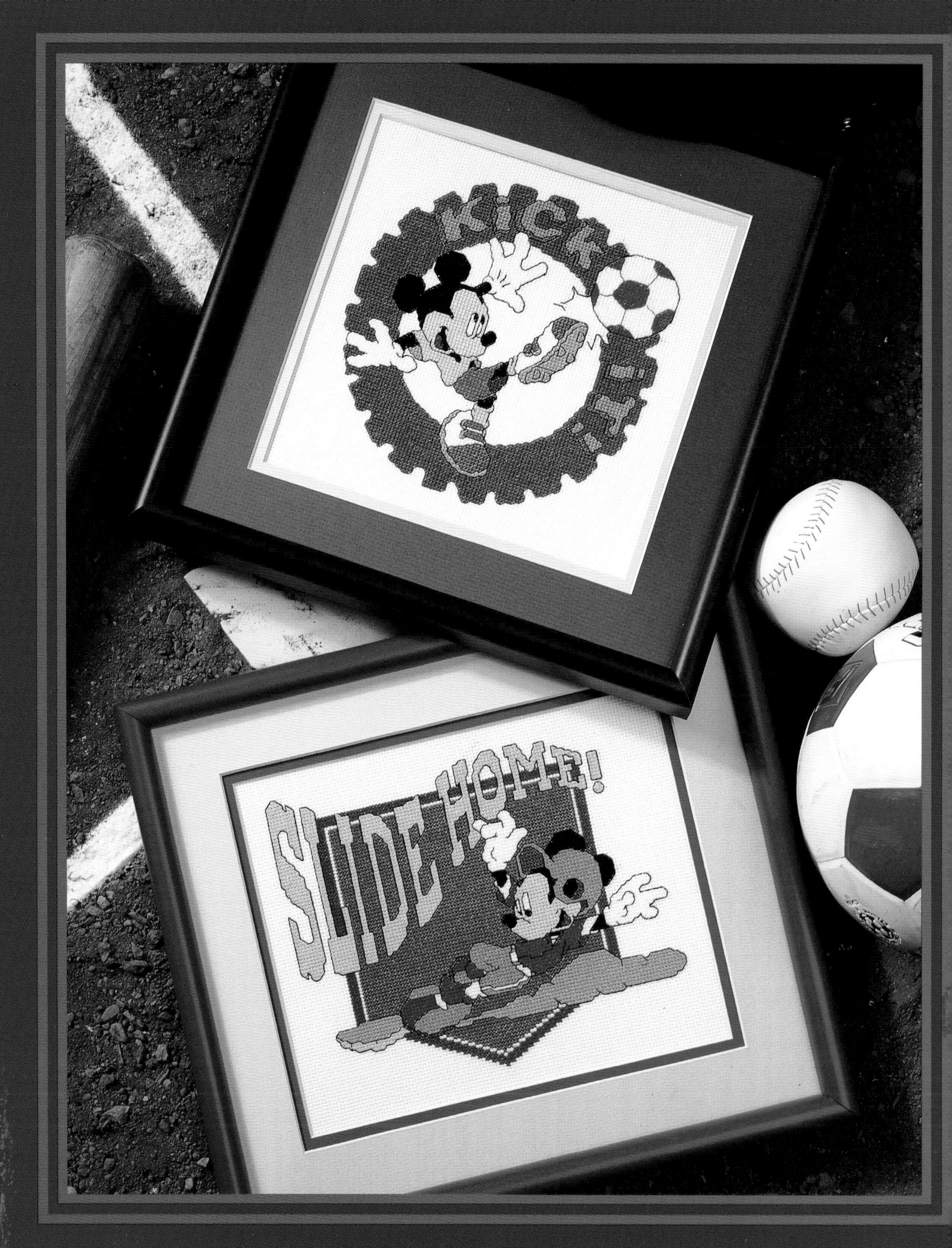

Charts on pages 78-79 and 82-83

harts on pages 74-77 and 80-81

Charts on pages 88-9

harts on pages 84-89

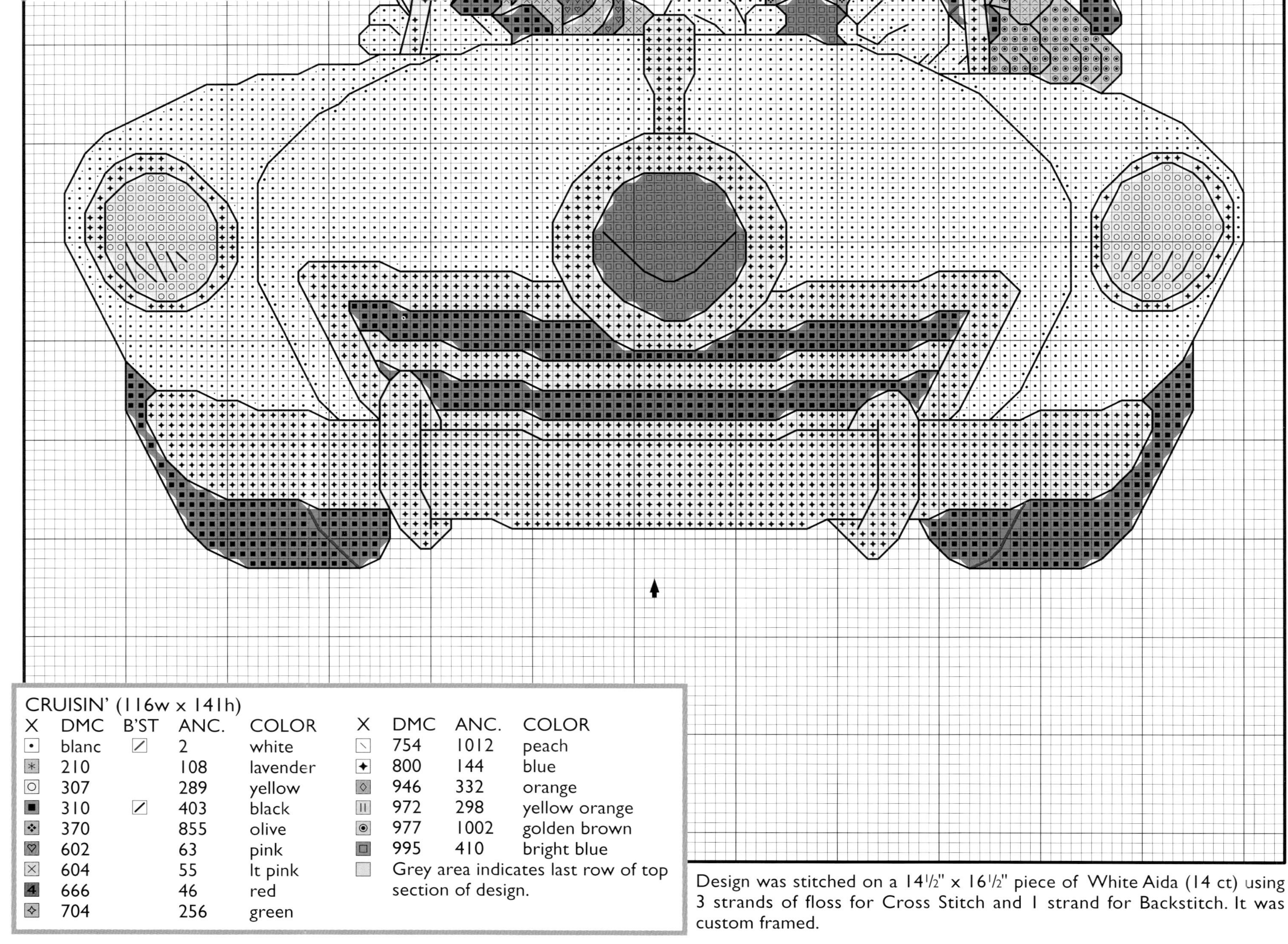

CRUISIN' (116w x 141h)

X	DMC	B'ST	ANC.	COLOR
•	blanc	/	2	white
✳	210		108	lavender
○	307		289	yellow
■	310	/	403	black
❖	370		855	olive
♡	602		63	pink
×	604		55	lt pink
4	666		46	red
✧	704		256	green

X	DMC	ANC.	COLOR
\	754	1012	peach
✦	800	144	blue
◇	946	332	orange
II	972	298	yellow orange
◉	977	1002	golden brown
□	995	410	bright blue
	Grey area indicates last row of top section of design.		

Design was stitched on a 14½" x 16½" piece of White Aida (14 ct) using 3 strands of floss for Cross Stitch and 1 strand for Backstitch. It was custom framed.

GO GET 'EM (75w x 110h)

X	DMC	B'ST	ANC.	COLOR
•	blanc	⟋	2	white
	blanc	⟋*	2	white
■	310	⟋	403	black
★	666	⟋	46	red
○	743		302	yellow
☆	754		1012	peach
▲	797	⟋	132	blue
●	blanc		2	white Fr. Knot

* Use 2 strands of floss and long stitches.

Design was stitched on an 11½" x [illegible] piece of White Aida (14 ct) using 3 stra[illegible] of floss for Cross Stitch, 2 strands [illegible] French Knots, and 1 strand for Backsti[illegible] except where noted in color key. It w[illegible] custom framed.

'HAT CAN I SAY? (78w x 103h)

DMC	B'ST	ANC.	COLOR	X	DMC	B'ST	ANC.	COLOR
blanc	⁄*	2	white	▲	797	⁄†	132	blue
310	⁄	403	black	●	blanc		2	white Fr. Knot
666		46	red	●	797		132	blue Fr. Knot
743		302	yellow	* Use 3 strands of floss for wording.				
754		1012	peach	† Use 2 strands of floss.				

Design was stitched on a 12" x 13½" piece of White Aida (14 ct) using 3 strands of floss for Cross Stitch, 2 strands for French Knots, and 1 strand for Backstitch except where noted in color key. It was custom framed.

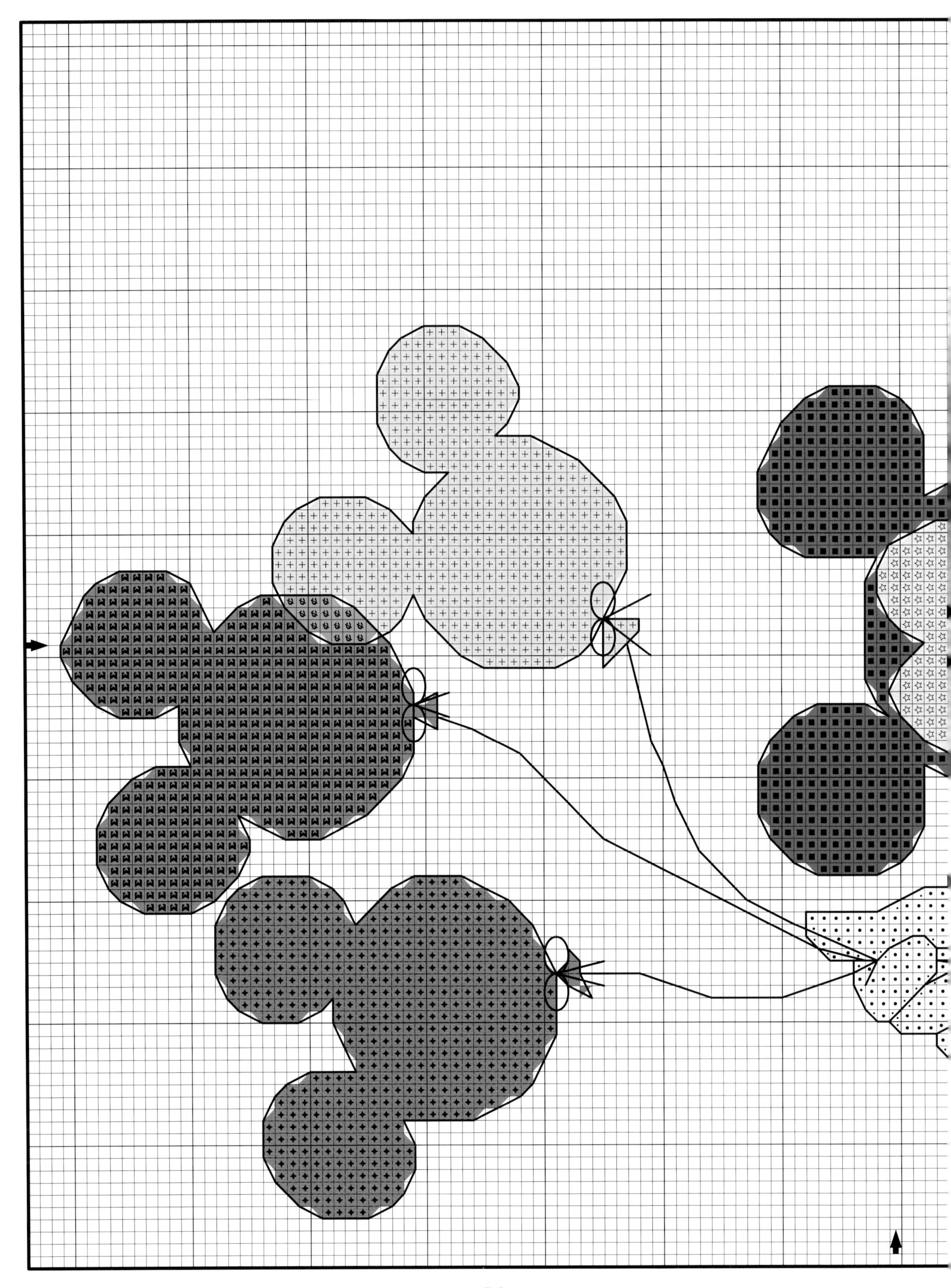

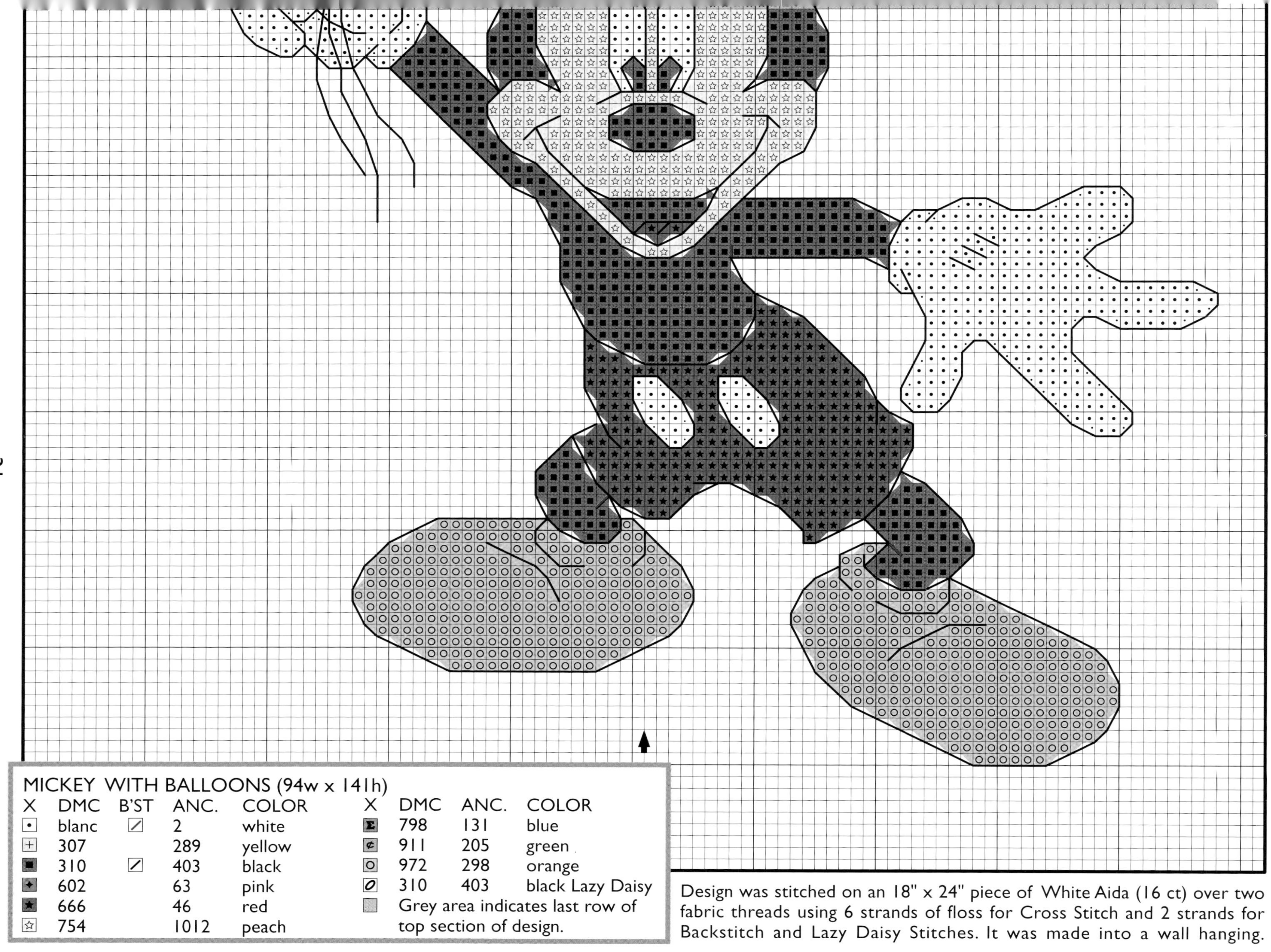

MICKEY WITH BALLOONS (94w x 141h)

X	DMC	B'ST	ANC.	COLOR
•	blanc	⁄	2	white
+	307		289	yellow
■	310	⁄	403	black
✦	602		63	pink
★	666		46	red
☆	754		1012	peach

X	DMC	ANC.	COLOR
Σ	798	131	blue
¢	911	205	green
O	972	298	orange
Ø	310	403	black Lazy Daisy
▢	Grey area indicates last row of top section of design.		

Design was stitched on an 18" x 24" piece of White Aida (16 ct) over two fabric threads using 6 strands of floss for Cross Stitch and 2 strands for Backstitch and Lazy Daisy Stitches. It was made into a wall hanging.

I LOVE MICKEY (101w x [illegible])

X	DMC	B'ST	ANC.	COLOR
•	blanc		2	white
■	310	⁄	403	black
★	666		46	red
○	743		302	yellow
☆	754		1012	peach
Σ	798		131	blue

Design was stitched on a 13½" x 12½" piece of White Aida (14 ct) using 3 strands of floss for Cross Stitch and 1 strand for Backstitch. It was made into a pillow.

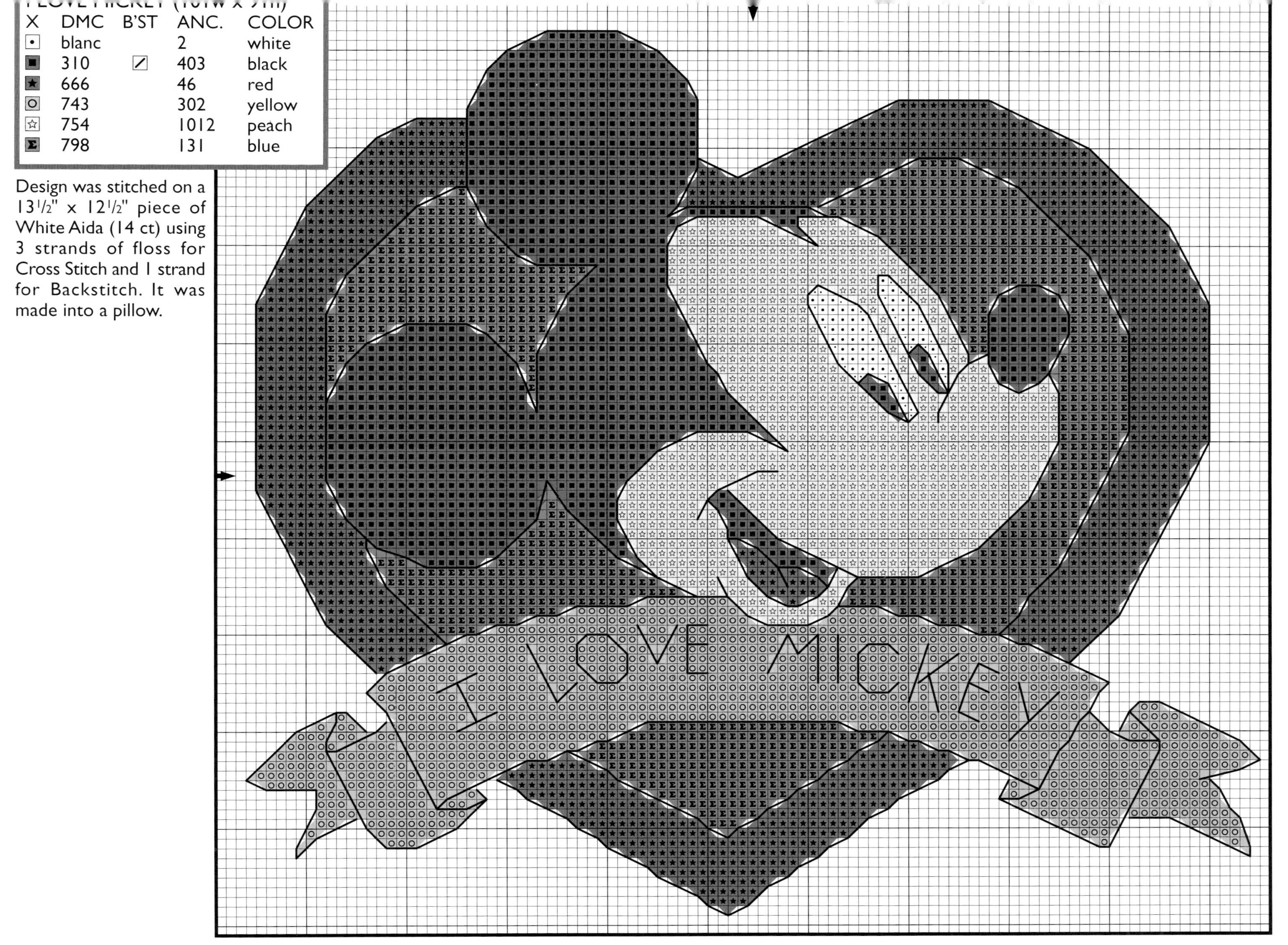

I LOVE MINNIE (101w x 91h)

X	DMC	B'ST	ANC.	COLOR
•	blanc		2	white
■	310	⁄	403	black
★	666		46	red
○	743		302	yellow
☆	754		1012	peach
Σ	798		131	blue
❖	3806		62	pink

Design was stitched on a 13½" x 12½" piece of White Aida (14 ct) using 3 strands of floss for Cross Stitch and 1 strand for Backstitch. It was custom framed.

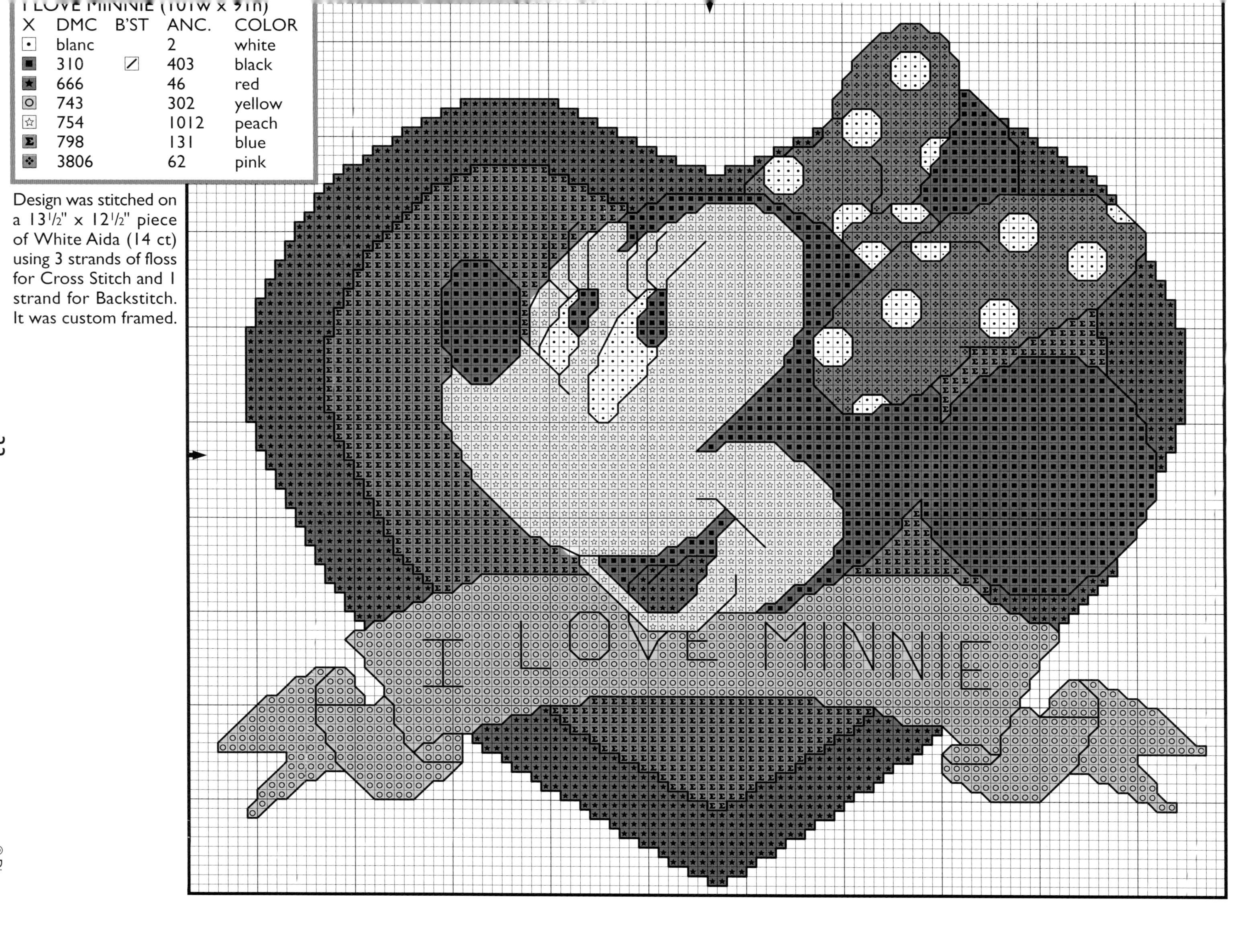

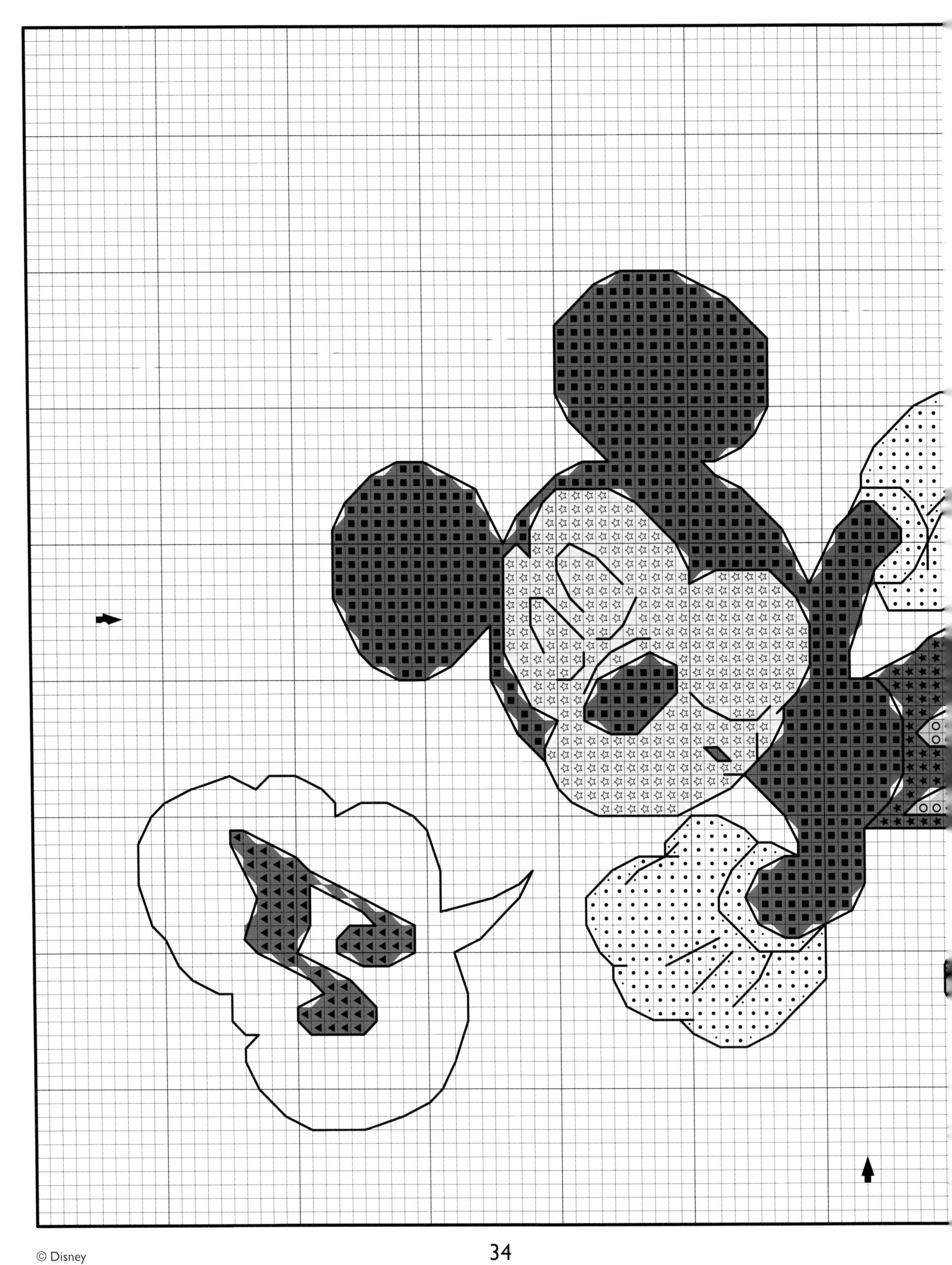

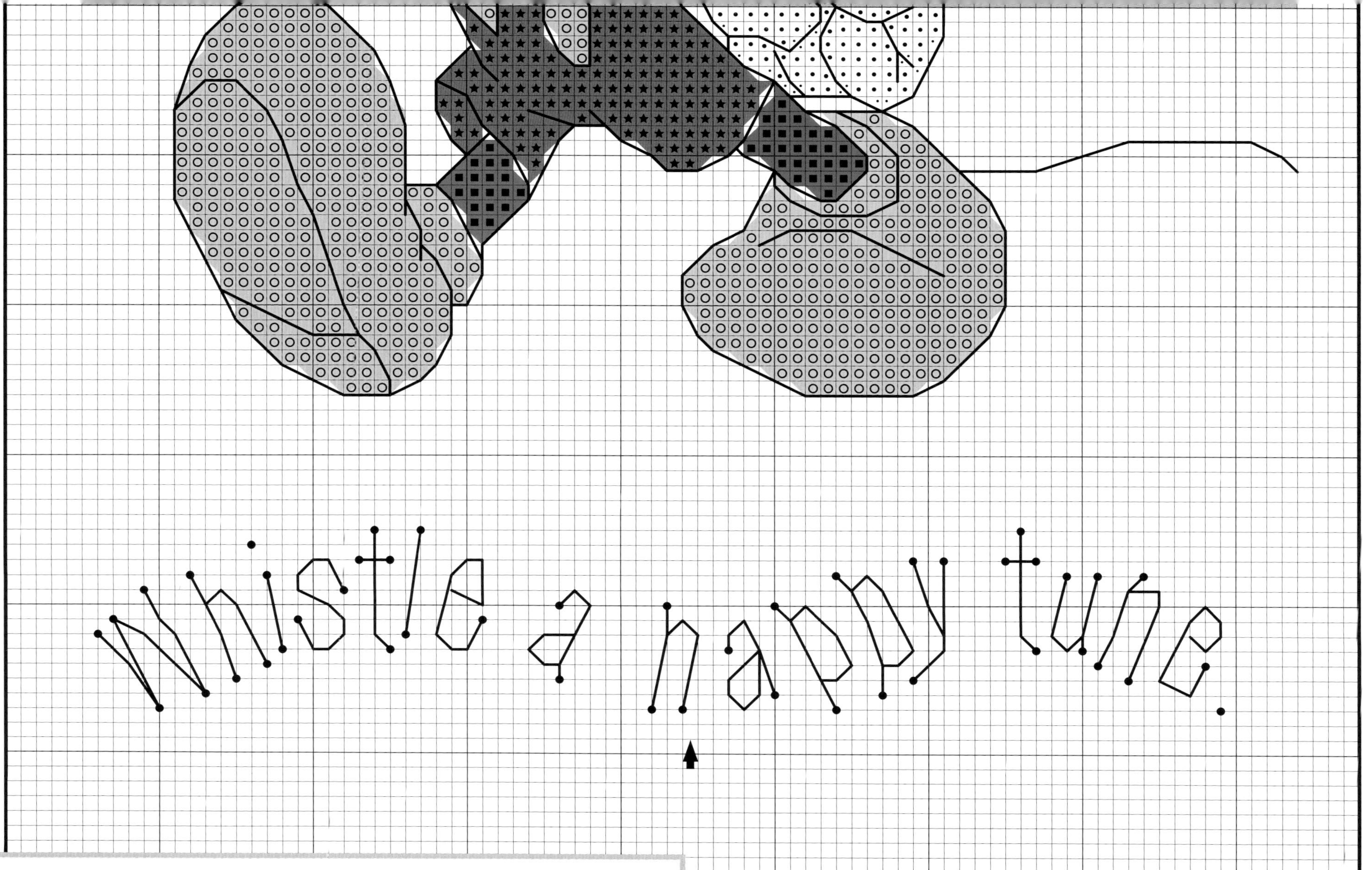

WHISTLE A HAPPY TUNE (79w x 110h)

X	DMC	B'ST	ANC.	COLOR
•	blanc		2	white
■	310	⁄	403	black
★	666		46	red
○	743		302	yellow
☆	754		1012	peach

X	DMC	ANC.	COLOR
▲	797	132	blue
●	310	403	black Fr. Knot
▢	Grey area indicates last row of top section of design.		

Design was stitched on a 12" x 14" piece of White Aida (14 ct) using 3 strands of floss for Cross Stitch, 2 strands for French Knots, and 1 strand for Backstitch. It was custom framed.

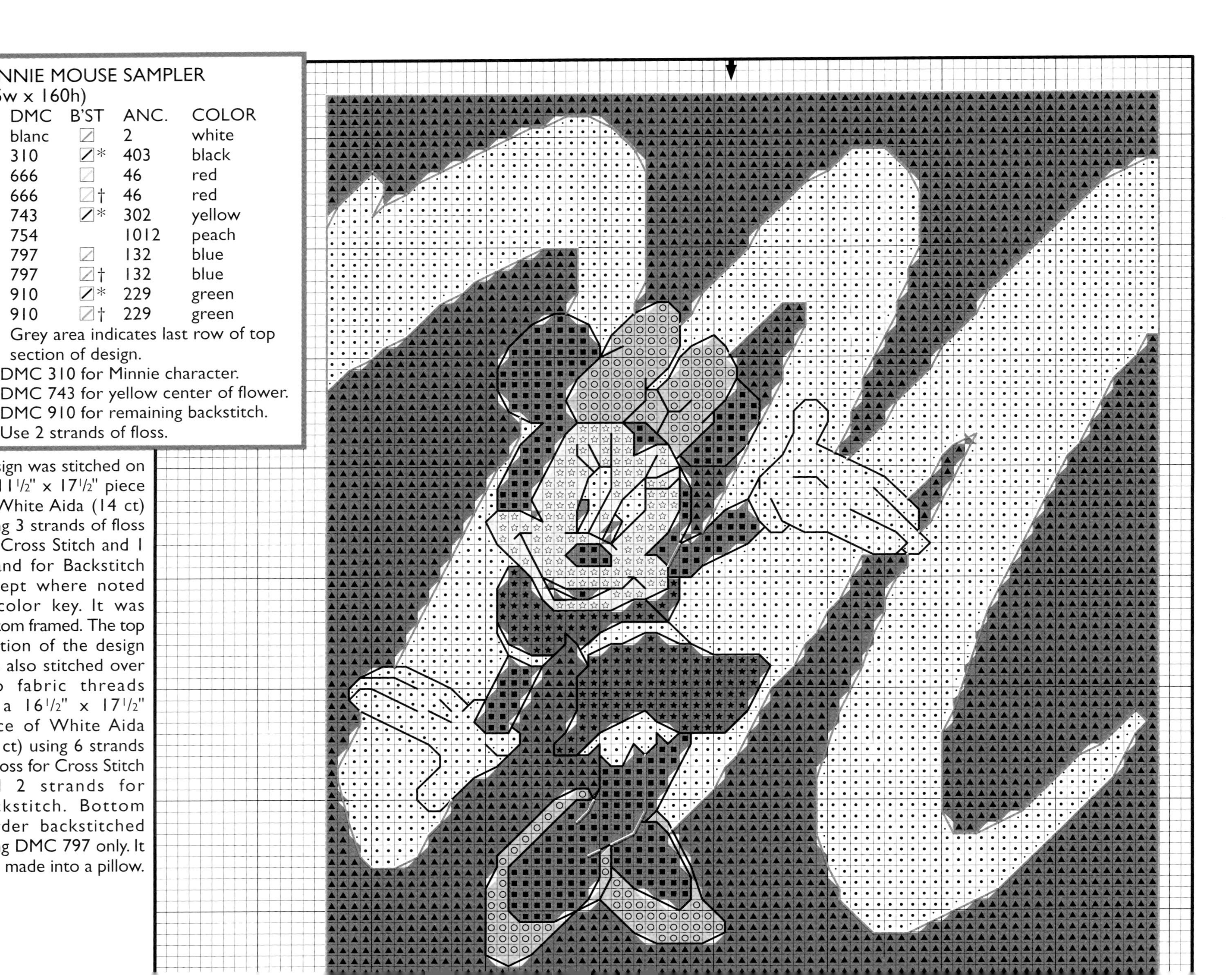

MINNIE MOUSE SAMPLER

(75w x 160h)

X	DMC	B'ST	ANC.	COLOR
•	blanc	◩	2	white
■	310	◩ *	403	black
★	666	◩	46	red
	666	◩ †	46	red
O	743	◩ *	302	yellow
☆	754		1012	peach
▲	797	◩	132	blue
	797	◩ †	132	blue
¢	910	◩ *	229	green
	910	◩ †	229	green

Grey area indicates last row of top section of design.

* DMC 310 for Minnie character.
DMC 743 for yellow center of flower.
DMC 910 for remaining backstitch.

† Use 2 strands of floss.

Design was stitched on an 11½" x 17½" piece of White Aida (14 ct) using 3 strands of floss for Cross Stitch and 1 strand for Backstitch except where noted in color key. It was custom framed. The top portion of the design was also stitched over two fabric threads on a 16½" x 17½" piece of White Aida (14 ct) using 6 strands of floss for Cross Stitch and 2 strands for Backstitch. Bottom border backstitched using DMC 797 only. It was made into a pillow.

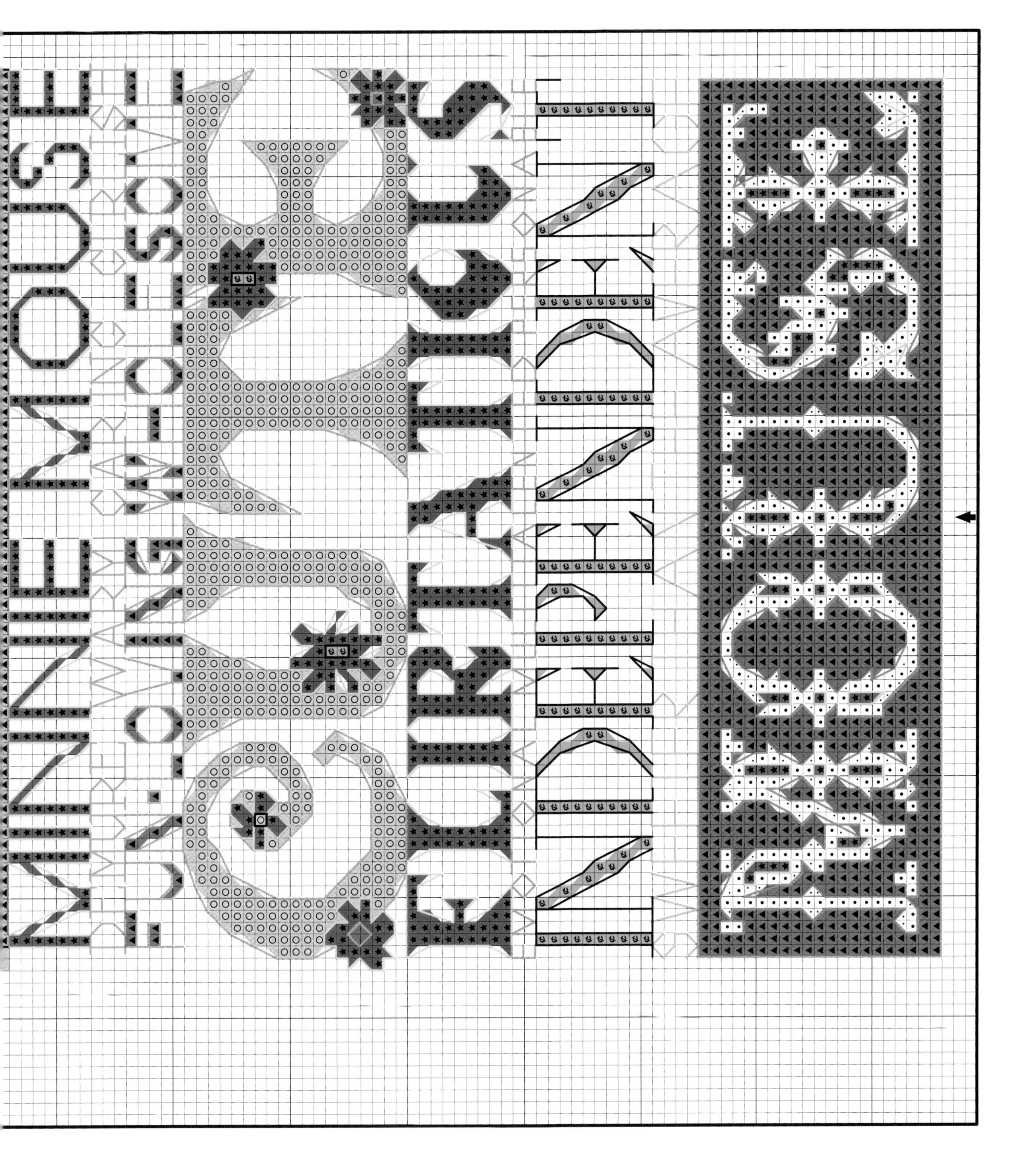

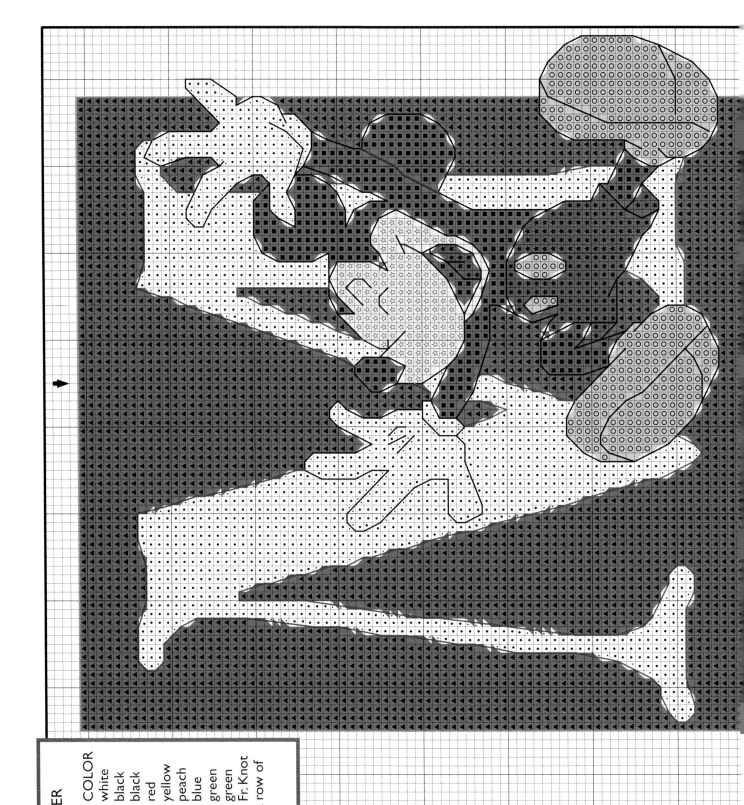

MICKEY MOUSE SAMPLER
(80w x 159h)

X	DMC	B'ST	ANC.	COLOR
•	blanc	⟋	2	white
■	310	⟋	403	black
	310	⟋*	403	black
★	666	⟋	46	red
○	743		302	yellow
☆	754		1012	peach
▲	797	⟋	132	blue
¢	910	⟋	229	green
●	910		229	green Fr. Knot

▢ Grey area indicates last row of top section of design.

* Use 2 strands of floss.

Design was stitched on a 12" x 17½" piece of White Aida (14 ct) using 3 strands of floss for Cross Stitch and 1 strand for Backstitch and French Knots except where noted in color key. It was custom framed. The top portion of the design was also stitched over two fabric threads on a 17½" x 17½" piece of White Aida (14 ct) using 6 strands of floss for Cross Stitch and 2 strands for Backstitch. Bottom border backstitched with DMC 797 only. It was made into a pillow.

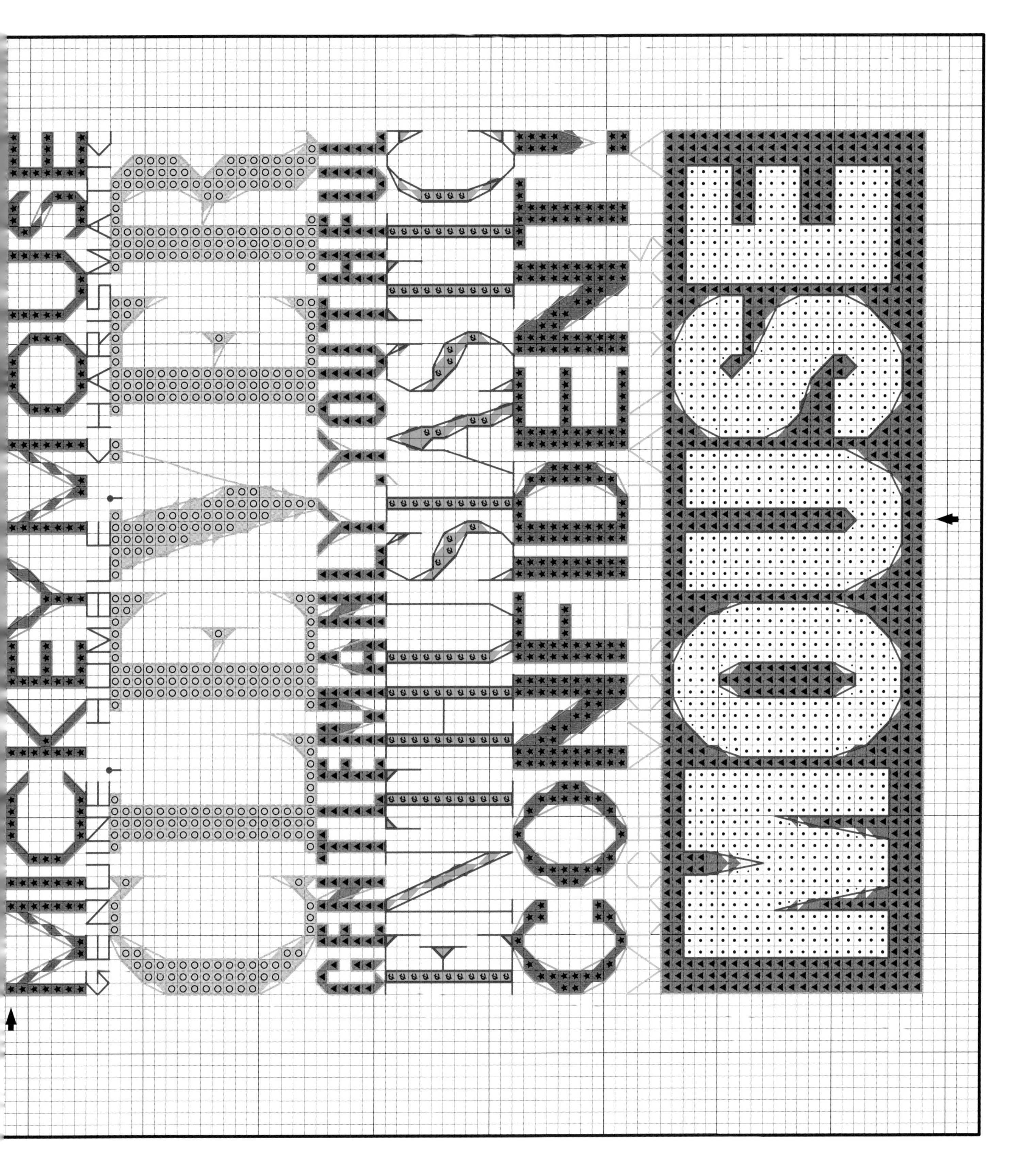
MICKEY MOUSE

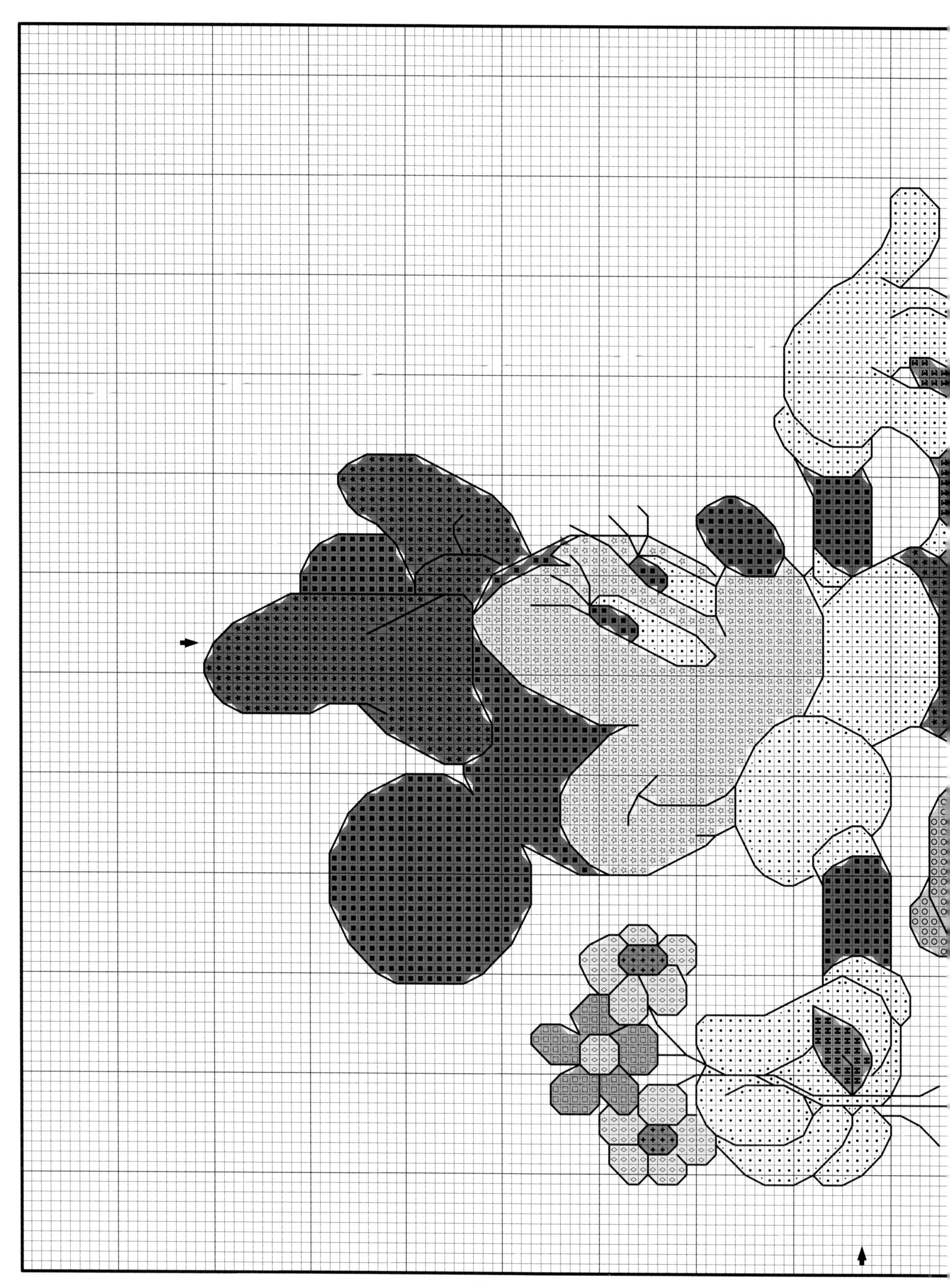

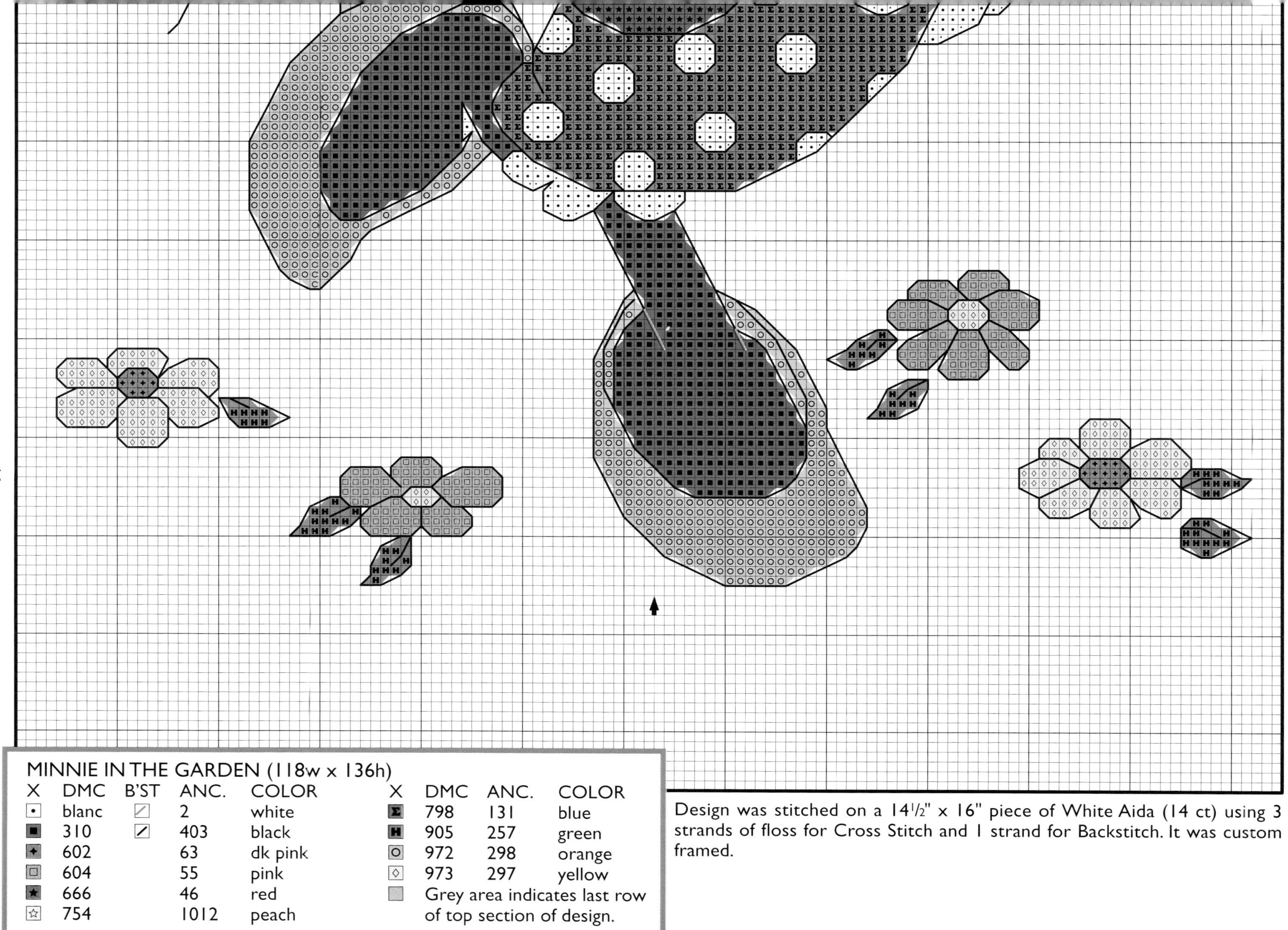

MINNIE IN THE GARDEN (118w x 136h)

X	DMC	B'ST	ANC.	COLOR
•	blanc	⟋	2	white
■	310	⟋	403	black
✦	602		63	dk pink
□	604		55	pink
★	666		46	red
☆	754		1012	peach

X	DMC	ANC.	COLOR
Σ	798	131	blue
H	905	257	green
O	972	298	orange
◊	973	297	yellow

Grey area indicates last row of top section of design.

Design was stitched on a 14½" x 16" piece of White Aida (14 ct) using 3 strands of floss for Cross Stitch and 1 strand for Backstitch. It was custom framed.

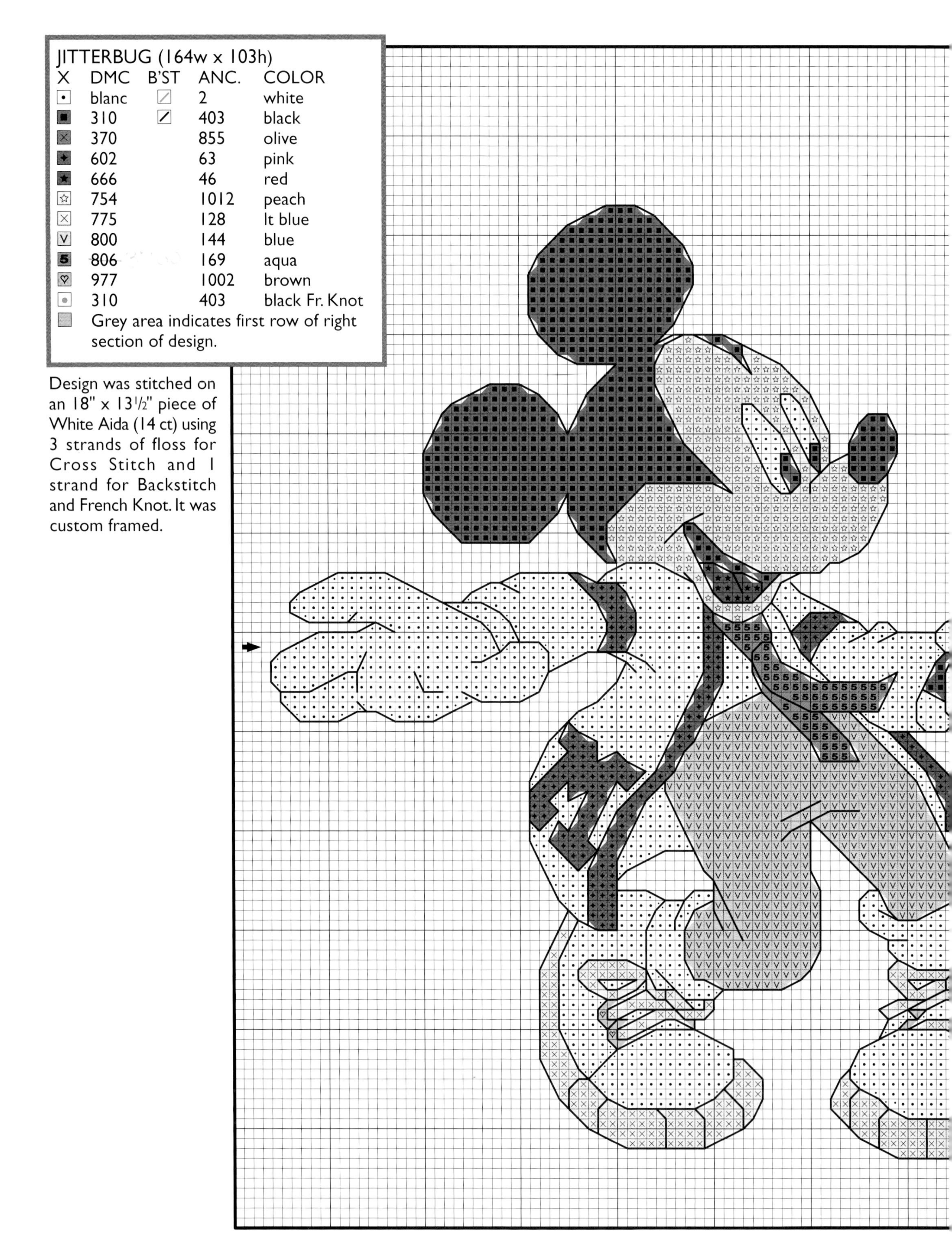

JITTERBUG (164w x 103h)

X	DMC	B'ST	ANC.	COLOR
	blanc		2	white
	310		403	black
	370		855	olive
	602		63	pink
	666		46	red
	754		1012	peach
	775		128	lt blue
	800		144	blue
	806		169	aqua
	977		1002	brown
	310		403	black Fr. Knot
	Grey area indicates first row of right section of design.			

Design was stitched on an 18" x 13½" piece of White Aida (14 ct) using 3 strands of floss for Cross Stitch and 1 strand for Backstitch and French Knot. It was custom framed.

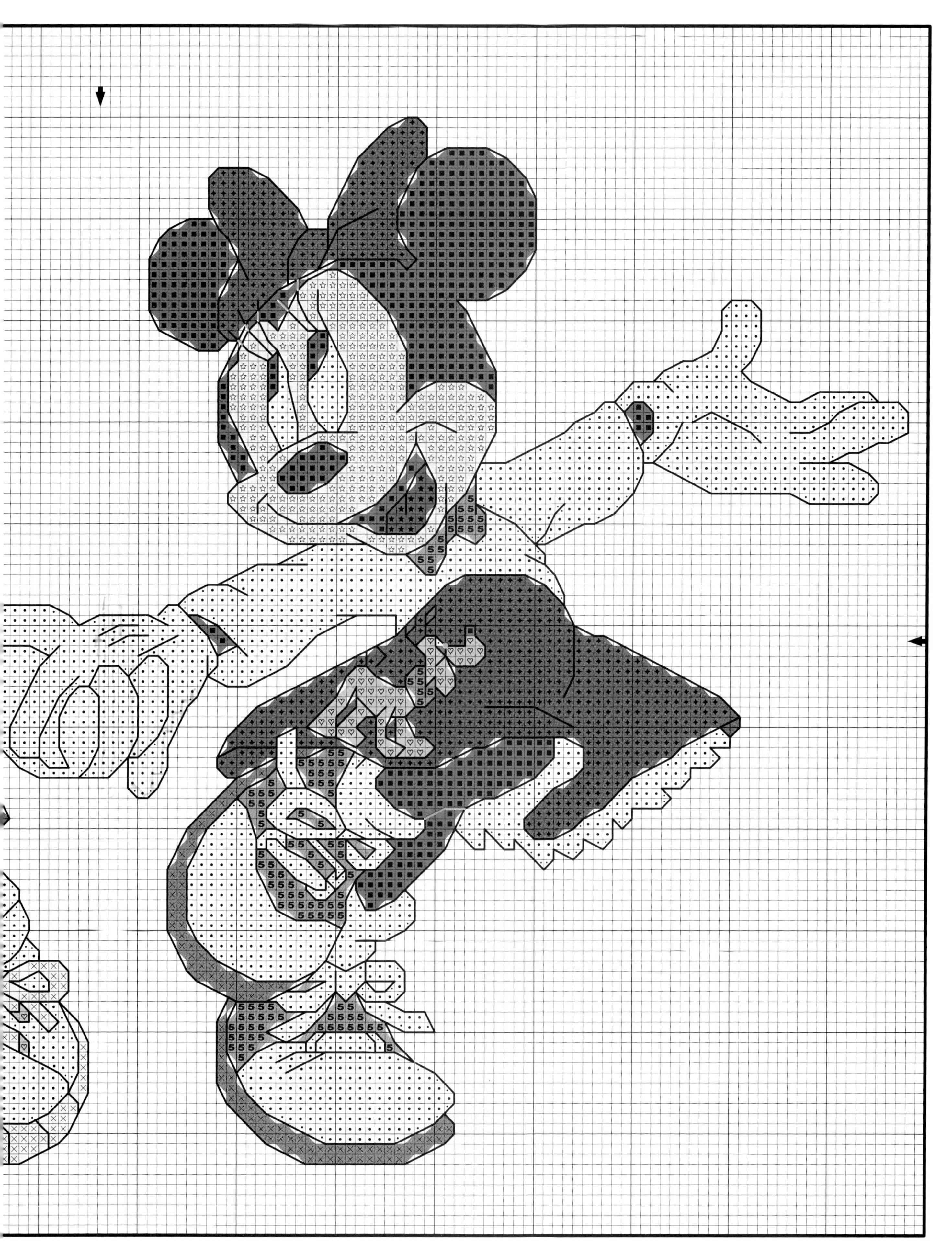

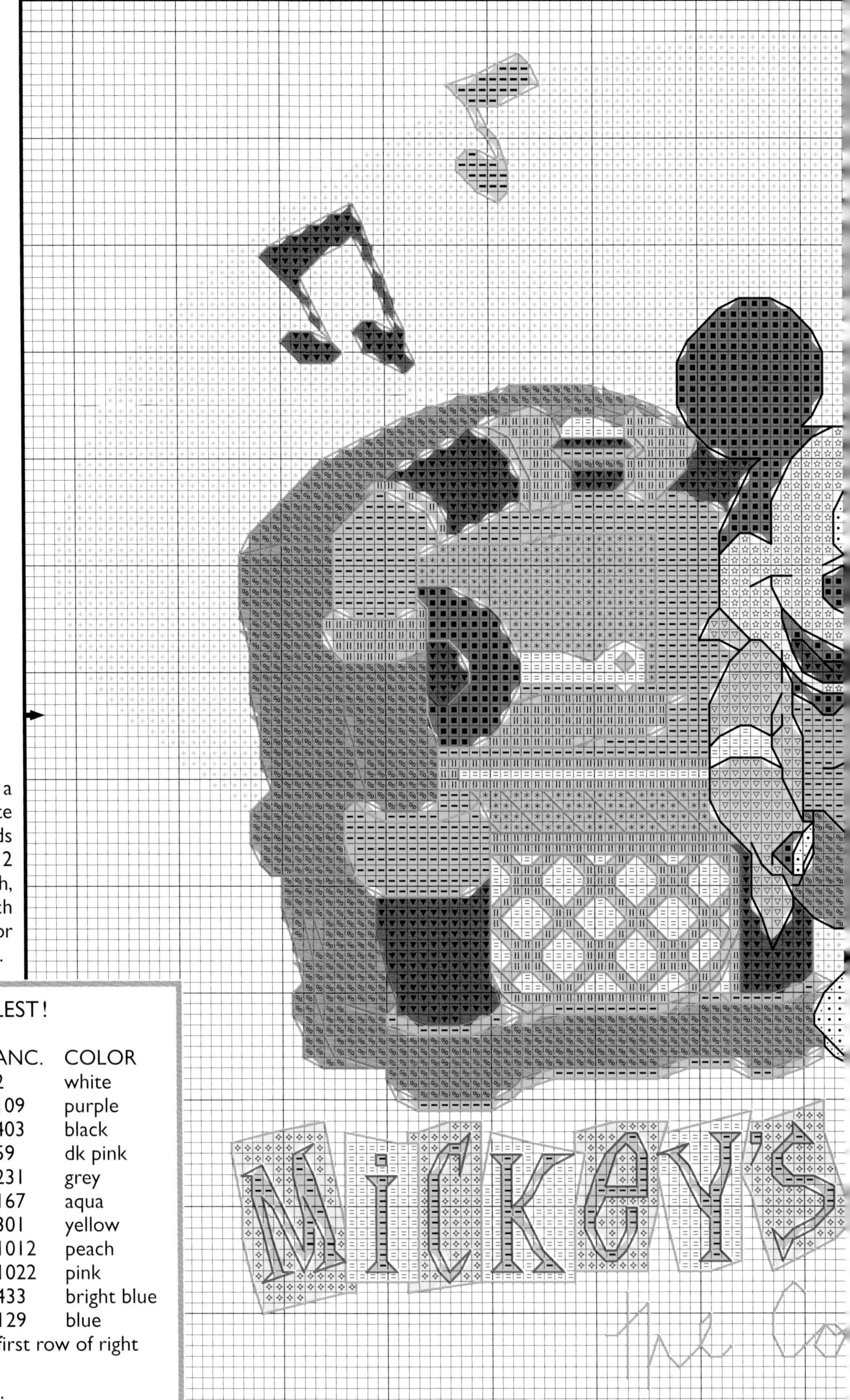

Design was stitched on a 19" x 15½" piece of White Aida (14 ct) using 3 strands of floss for Cross Stitch, 2 strands for Half Cross Stitch, and 1 strand for Backstitch except where noted in color key. It was custom framed.

MICKEY'S THE COOLEST!
(178w x 128h)

X	DMC	½X	B'ST	ANC.	COLOR
•	blanc			2	white
%	209			109	purple
■	310		/	403	black
▼	326		/ *	59	dk pink
II	453			231	grey
✧	598	✧		167	aqua
=	744			301	yellow
☆	754			1012	peach
*	760			1022	pink
–	996		/	433	bright blue
▽	3325			129	blue

Grey area indicates first row of right section of design.

* Use 2 strands of floss.

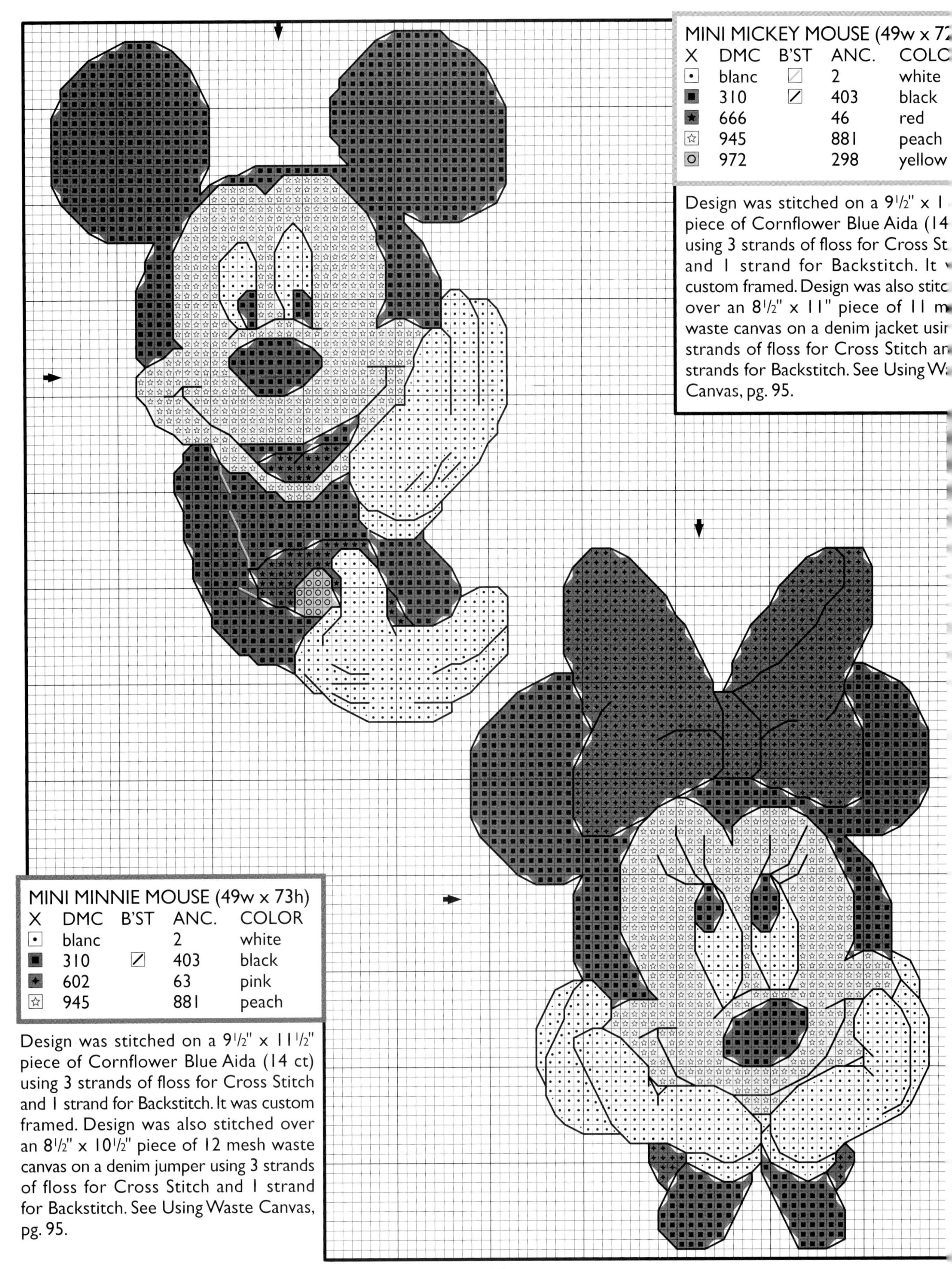

MINI MICKEY MOUSE (49w x 7

X	DMC	B'ST	ANC.	COLO
•	blanc	⁄	2	white
■	310	⁄	403	black
★	666		46	red
☆	945		881	peach
○	972		298	yellow

Design was stitched on a 9½" x 1 piece of Cornflower Blue Aida (14 using 3 strands of floss for Cross St and 1 strand for Backstitch. It custom framed. Design was also stitc over an 8½" x 11" piece of 11 m waste canvas on a denim jacket usir strands of floss for Cross Stitch ar strands for Backstitch. See Using W Canvas, pg. 95.

MINI MINNIE MOUSE (49w x 73h)

X	DMC	B'ST	ANC.	COLOR
•	blanc		2	white
■	310	⁄	403	black
✦	602		63	pink
☆	945		881	peach

Design was stitched on a 9½" x 11½" piece of Cornflower Blue Aida (14 ct) using 3 strands of floss for Cross Stitch and 1 strand for Backstitch. It was custom framed. Design was also stitched over an 8½" x 10½" piece of 12 mesh waste canvas on a denim jumper using 3 strands of floss for Cross Stitch and 1 strand for Backstitch. See Using Waste Canvas, pg. 95.

AUTOGRAPH MICKEY MOUSE (73w x 105h)

X	DMC	B'ST	ANC.	COLOR
•	blanc		2	white
■	310	/	403	black
★	666	/ *	46	red
☆	945		881	peach
○	972		298	yellow

* Use long stitches.

Design was stitched over two fabric threads on a 16½" x 21" piece of White Aida (14 ct) using 6 strands of floss for Cross Stitch and Backstitch wording and 2 strands for remaining Backstitch. It was made into a wall hanging.

PLUTO IN THE DOG HOUSE (100w x 89h)

X	DMC	B'ST	ANC.	COLOR
•	blanc	/	2	white
■	310	/	403	black
★	666		46	red
♦	704		256	green
♡	977		1002	brown
Π	3708		31	pink
	Grey area indicates first row of right section of design.			

Design was stitched on a 13½" x 12½" piece of White Aida (14 ct) using 3 strands of floss for Cross Stitch and 1 strand for Backstitch. It was custom framed.

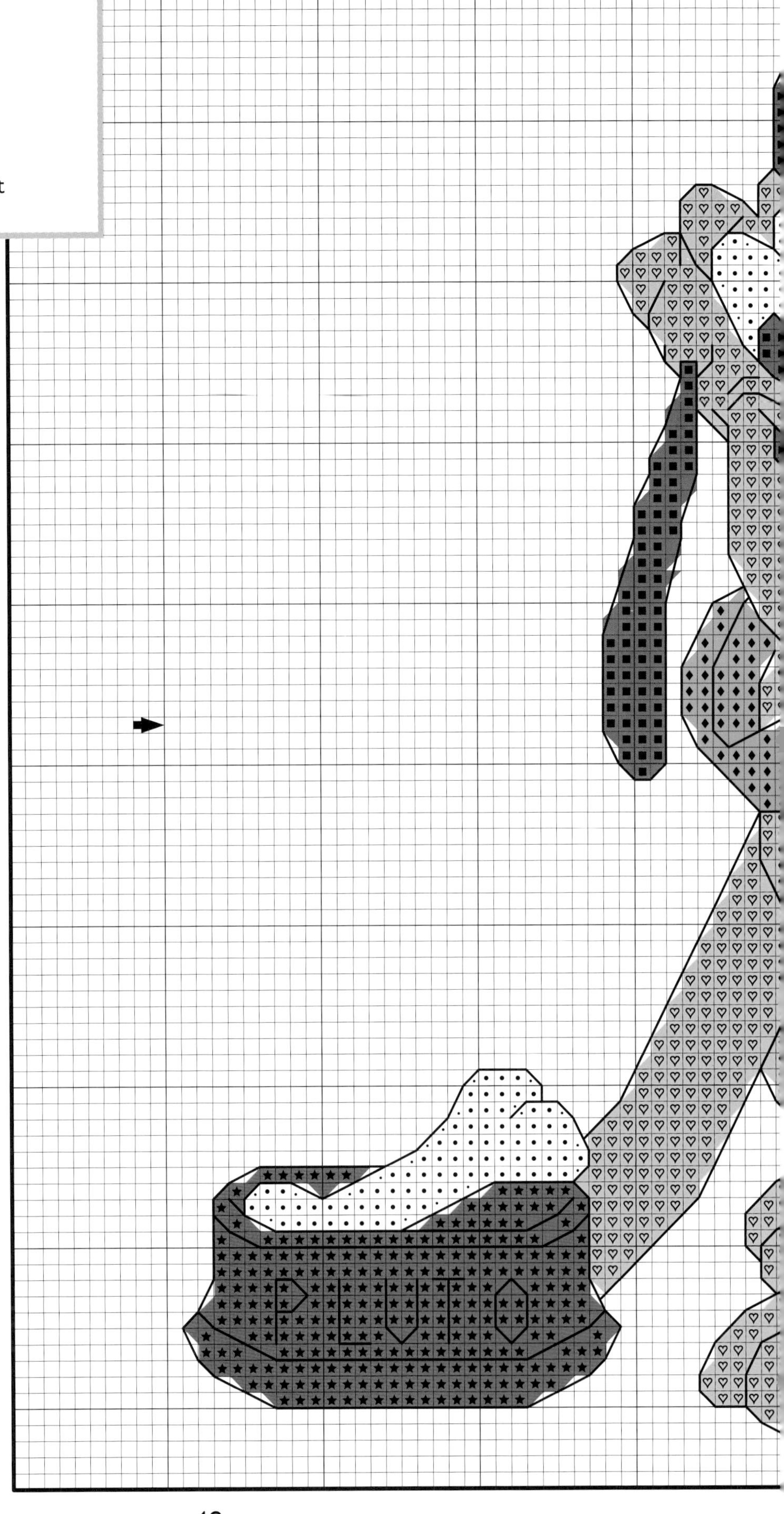

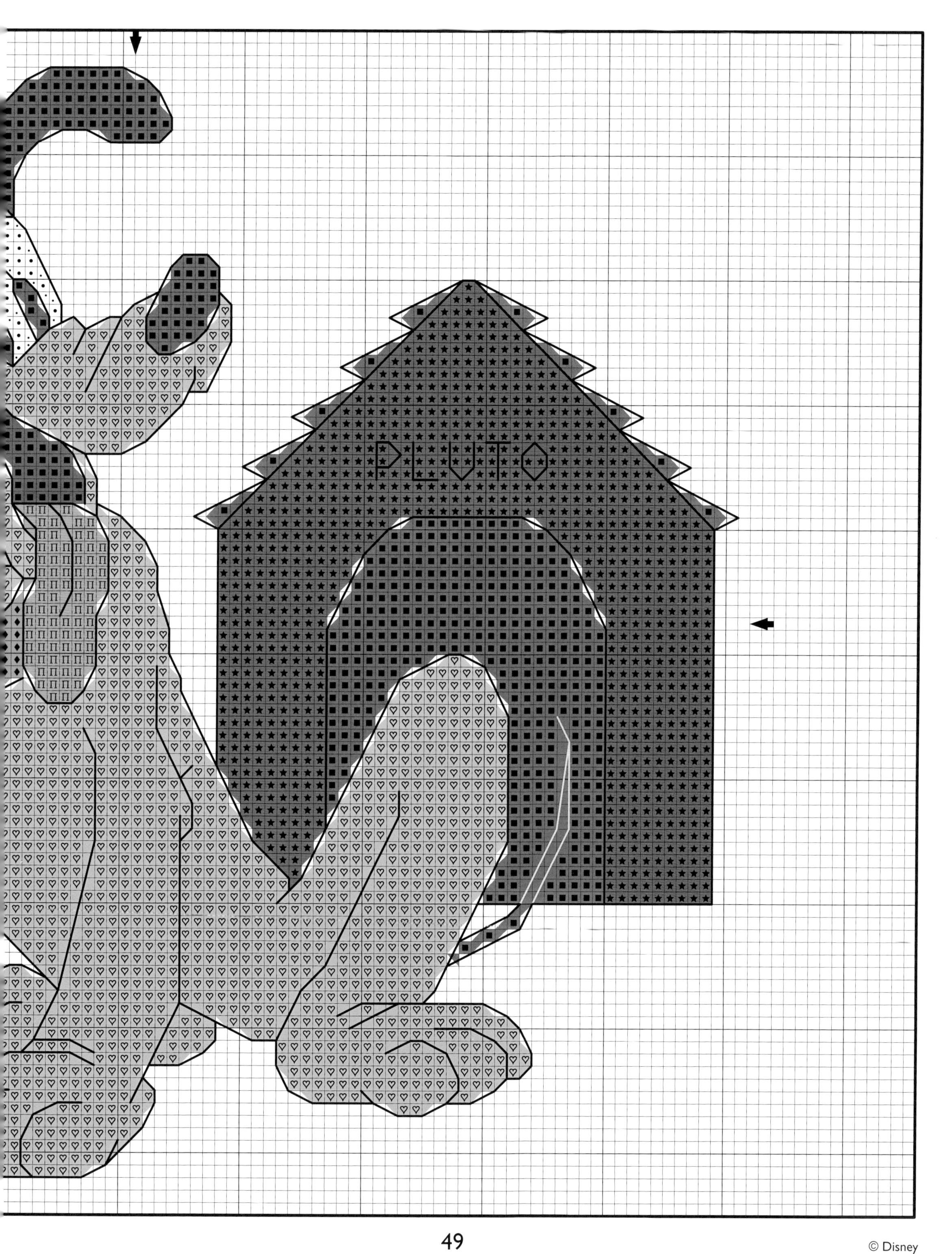
PLUTO

THE GANG'S ALL HERE
(160w x 106h)

X	DMC	B'ST	ANC.	COLOR
•	blanc	⁄	2	white
⊕	210		108	lt purple
■	310	⁄	403	black
□	604		55	pink
★	666	⁄	46	red
♦	704		256	green
V	800		144	lt blue
☆	945		881	peach
♥	946		332	orange
O	972		298	yellow
♡	977		1002	gold
H	995		410	dk blue
–	996		433	blue
✔	3746		1030	purple
❖	3806		62	dk pink
	Grey area indicates first row of right section of design.			

Design was stitched on a 17½" x 14" piece of White Aida (14 ct) using 3 strands of floss for Cross Stitch and 1 strand for Backstitch. It was custom framed. The design was also stitched, omitting words, over two fabric threads at the bottom of a White All-Cotton Anne Cloth Afghan using 6 strands of floss for Cross Stitch and 2 strands for Backstitch.

ng's all here

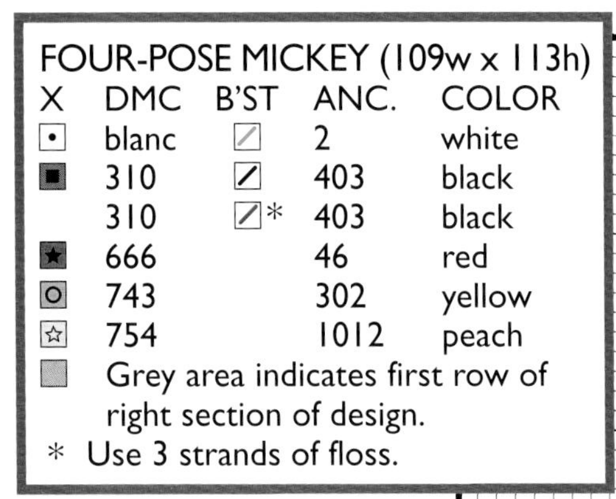

FOUR-POSE MICKEY (109w x 113h)

X	DMC	B'ST	ANC.	COLOR
•	blanc	⁄	2	white
■	310	⁄	403	black
	310	⁄ *	403	black
★	666		46	red
O	743		302	yellow
☆	754		1012	peach
▒	Grey area indicates first row of right section of design.			

* Use 3 strands of floss.

Design was stitched on a 14" x 14½" piece of White Aida (14 ct) using 3 strands of floss for Cross Stitch and 1 strand for Backstitch except where noted in color key. It was custom framed. The design was also stitched omitting words on White Aida (14 ct) using 3 strands of floss for Cross Stitch and 1 strand for Backstitch. It was adhered to a cross stitch mouse pad. The words only were stitched on White Vinyl-Weave™ (14 ct) using 3 strands of floss for Backstitch and inserted into a plastic cross stitch ruler. The bottom head and left head only were each stitched on White Vinyl-Weave (14 ct) using 3 strands of floss for Cross Stitch and 1 strand for Backstitch and inserted into a plastic cross stitch letter opener and clip. The right Mickey only was stitched on White Vinyl-Weave (14 ct) using 3 strands of floss for Cross Stitch and 1 strand for Backstitch and inserted into a plastic cross stitch caddy.

EY MOUSE

COLOR BLOCKS (150w x 100h)

X	DMC	B'ST	ANC.	COLOR
•	blanc	⁄	2	white
■	310	⁄	403	black
◉	340		118	periwinkle
✦	602		63	pink
□	604		55	lt pink
★	666		46	red
♦	704		256	green
☆	754		1012	peach
V	800		144	blue
5	806		169	turquoise
⬟	814		45	maroon
♥	946		332	orange
◣	958		187	aqua
O	972		298	yellow
♡	977		1002	brown
•	310		403	black Fr. Knot
▒	Grey area indicates first row of right section of design.			

Design was stitched on a 17" x 13½" piece of White Aida (14 ct) using 3 strands of floss for Cross Stitch, 2 strands for French Knots, and 1 strand for Backstitch. It was custom framed. Characters were also stitched on a White All-Cotton Anne Cloth Afghan following diagram below. Designs were stitched over two fabric threads using 6 strands of floss for Cross Stitch, 4 strands for French Knots, and 2 strands for Backstitch. Mickey Mouse, Minnie Mouse, Donald Duck, and Daisy Duck were each stitched on Vinyl-Weave™ (14 ct) using 3 strands of floss for Cross Stitch and 1 strand for Backstitch and placed in plastic cross stitch coasters. Goofy and Pluto were each stitched on Vinyl-Weave (14 ct) using 3 strands of floss for Cross Stitch, 2 strands for French Knots, and 1 strand for Backstitch and placed in plastic cross stitch coolers.

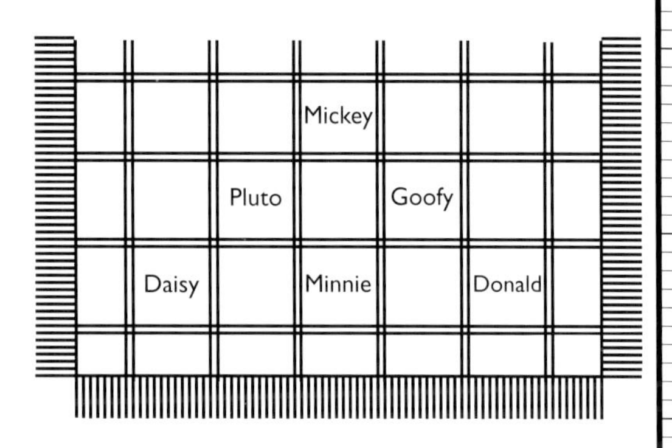

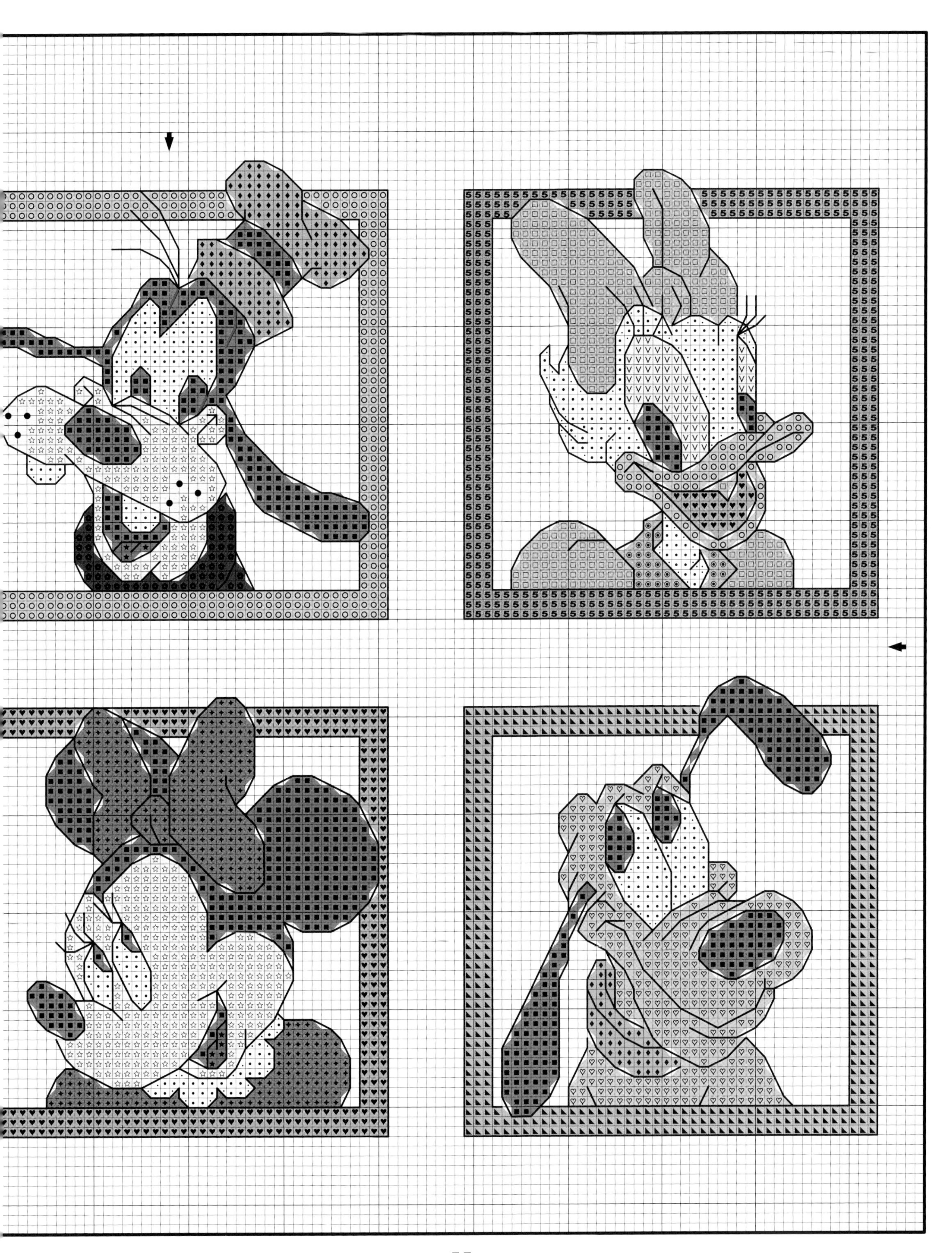

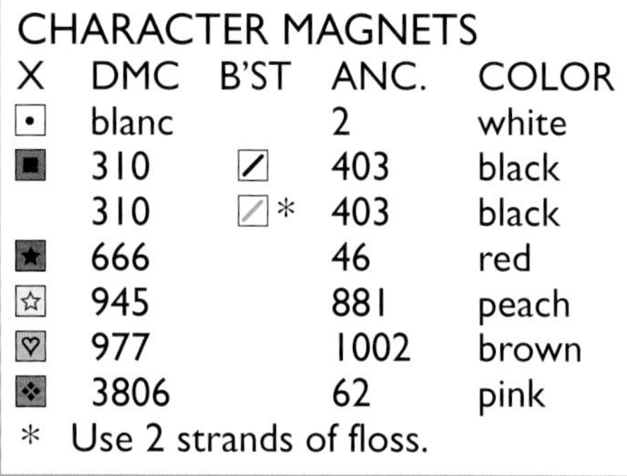

CHARACTER MAGNETS

X	DMC	B'ST	ANC.	COLOR
•	blanc		2	white
■	310	/	403	black
	310	/ *	403	black
★	666		46	red
☆	945		881	peach
♡	977		1002	brown
❖	3806		62	pink

* Use 2 strands of floss.

Designs were stitched on 5" x 5" pieces of perforated plastic (14 ct) using 3 strands of floss for Cross Stitch and 1 strand for Backstitch except where noted in color key. They were made into magnets. Minnie Mouse was also stitched on Vinyl-Weave™ (14 ct) using 3 strands of floss for Cross Stitch and 1 strand for Backstitch except where noted in color key and placed in a plastic cross stitch cooler.

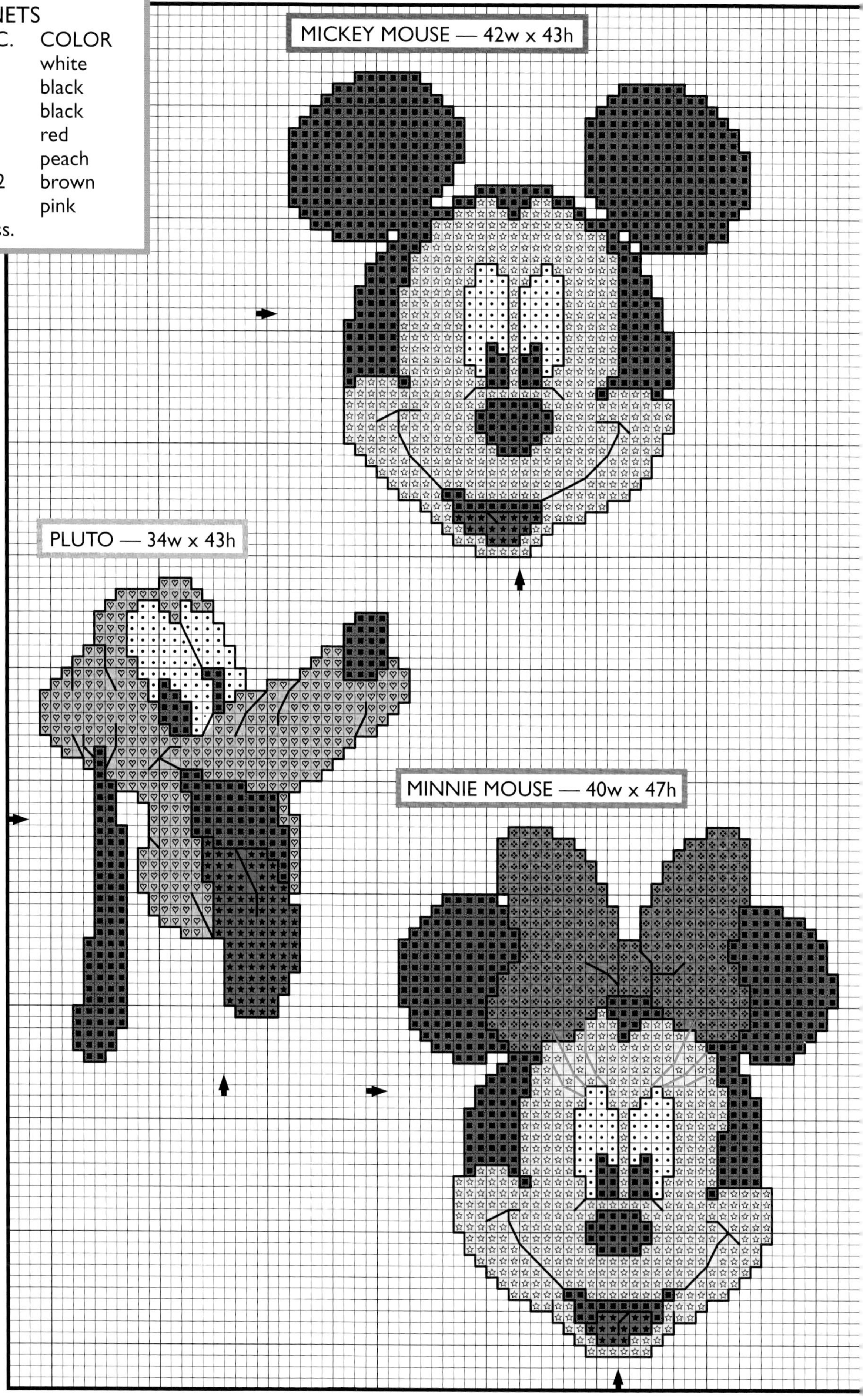

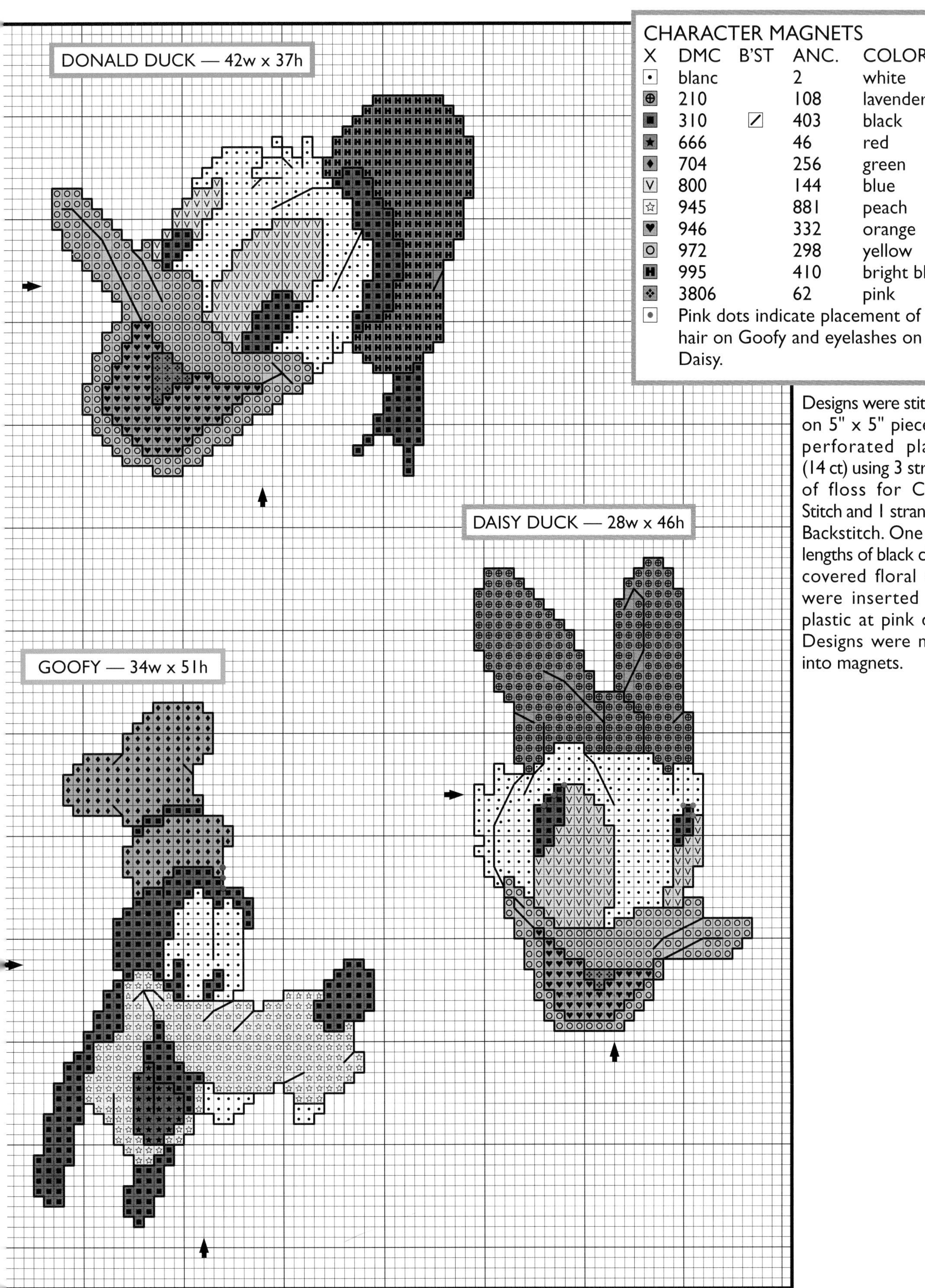

CHARACTER MAGNETS

X	DMC	B'ST	ANC.	COLOR
•	blanc		2	white
⊕	210		108	lavender
■	310	/	403	black
★	666		46	red
♦	704		256	green
V	800		144	blue
☆	945		881	peach
♥	946		332	orange
O	972		298	yellow
H	995		410	bright blue
❖	3806		62	pink
•	Pink dots indicate placement of hair on Goofy and eyelashes on Daisy.			

Designs were stitched on 5" x 5" pieces of perforated plastic (14 ct) using 3 strands of floss for Cross Stitch and 1 strand for Backstitch. One inch lengths of black cloth-covered floral wire were inserted into plastic at pink dots. Designs were made into magnets.

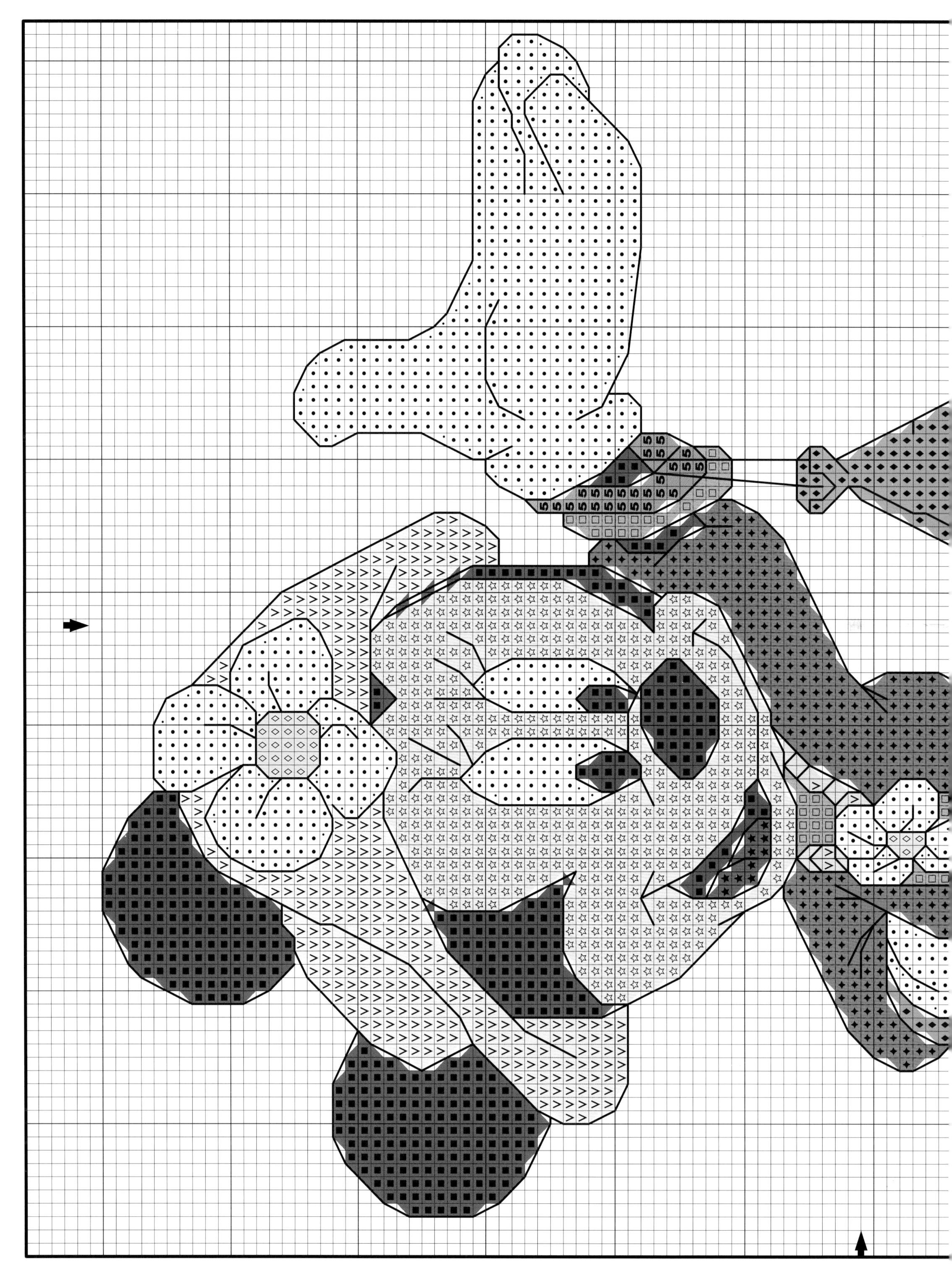

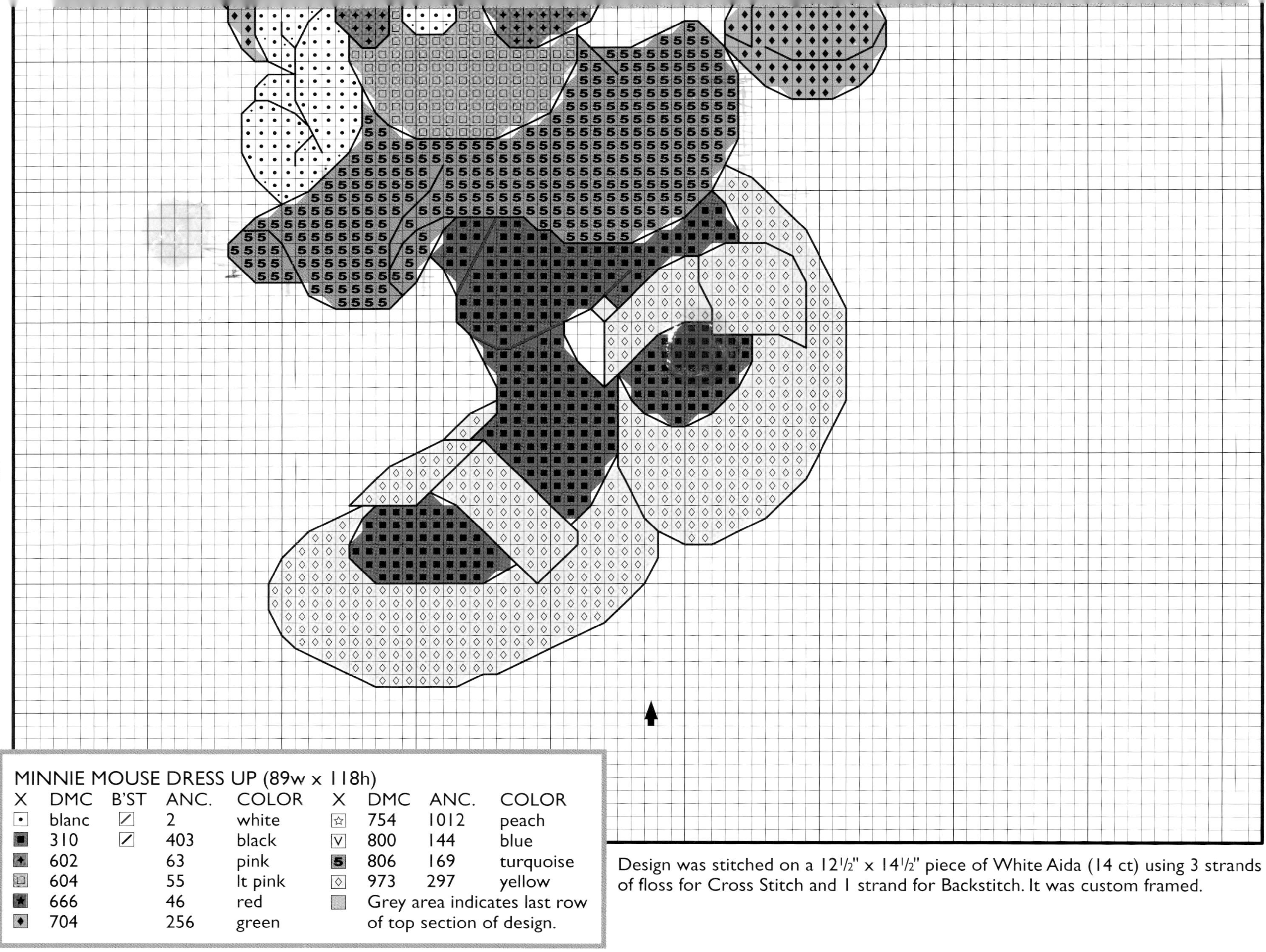

MINNIE MOUSE DRESS UP (89w x 118h)

X	DMC	B'ST	ANC.	COLOR
•	blanc	⁄	2	white
■	310	⁄	403	black
✦	602		63	pink
□	604		55	lt pink
★	666		46	red
♦	704		256	green

X	DMC	ANC.	COLOR
☆	754	1012	peach
V	800	144	blue
5	806	169	turquoise
◇	973	297	yellow

Grey area indicates last row of top section of design.

Design was stitched on a 12½" x 14½" piece of White Aida (14 ct) using 3 strands of floss for Cross Stitch and 1 strand for Backstitch. It was custom framed.

PHOTO SHOOT (132w x 110h)				
X	DMC	B'ST	ANC.	COLOR
•	blanc	⁄	2	white
■	310	⁄	403	black
$	415		398	grey
✦	602		63	pink
□	604		55	lt pink
★	666		46	red
☆	754		1012	peach
>	783		307	gold
Σ	798		131	blue
V	800		144	lt blue
◇	973		297	yellow
	Grey area indicates first row of right section of design.			

Design was stitched on a 15½" x 14" piece of White Aida (14 ct) using 3 strands of floss for Cross Stitch and 1strand for Backstitch. It was mounted on a fabric-covered photo album.

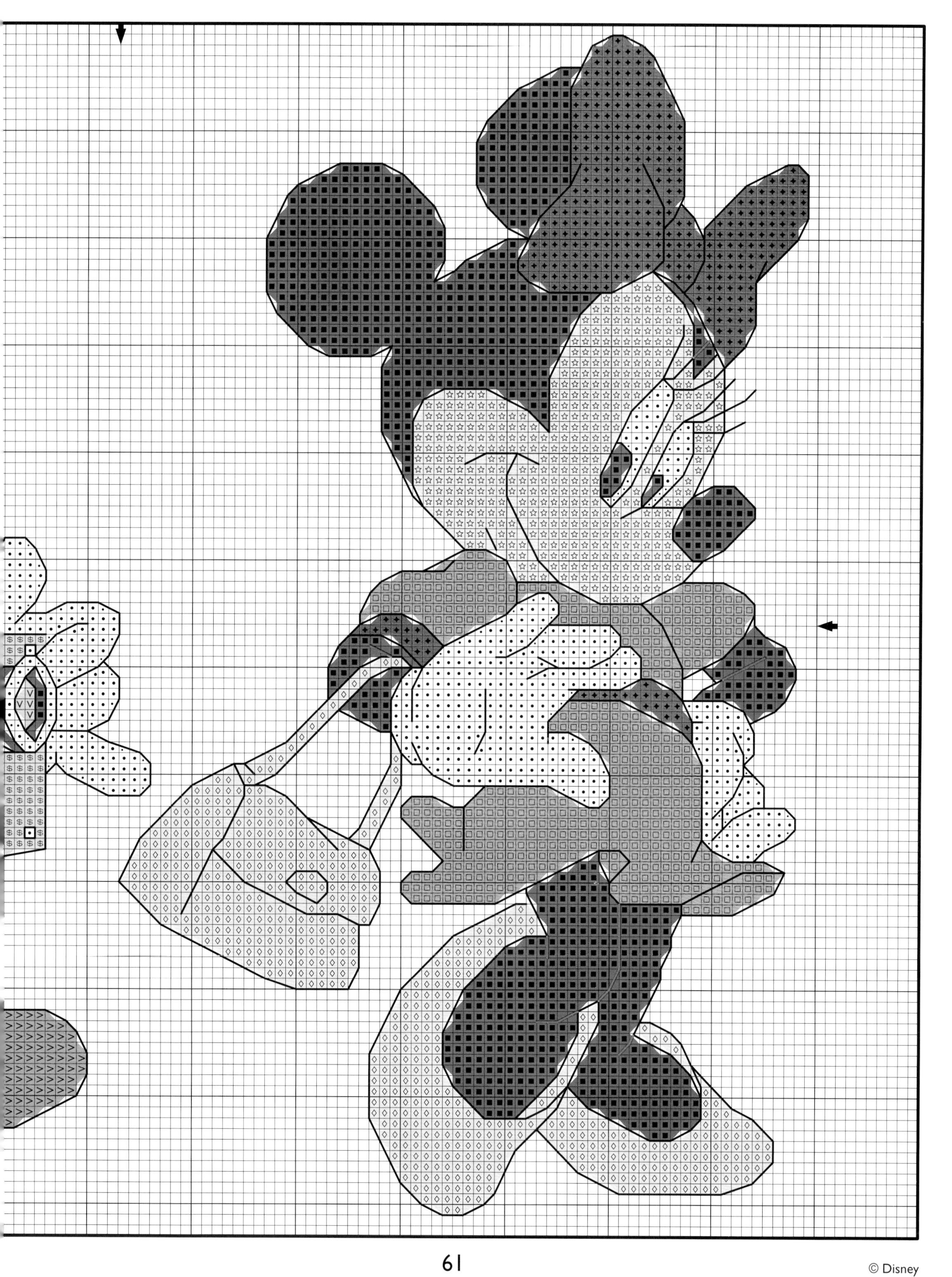

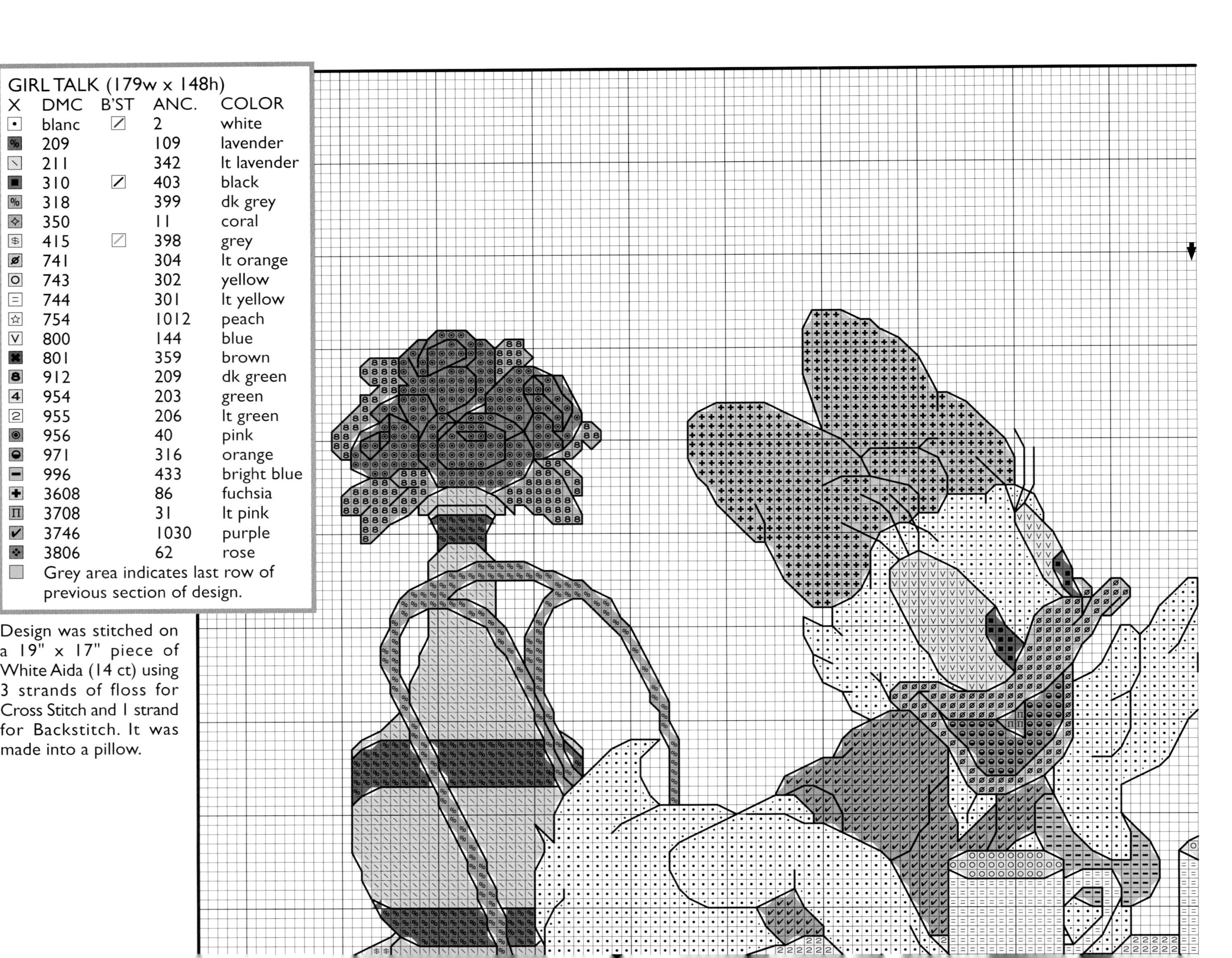

GIRL TALK (179w x 148h)

X	DMC	B'ST	ANC.	COLOR
•	blanc	/	2	white
%	209		109	lavender
\	211		342	lt lavender
■	310	/	403	black
%	318		399	dk grey
✧	350		11	coral
$	415	/	398	grey
ø	741		304	lt orange
O	743		302	yellow
=	744		301	lt yellow
☆	754		1012	peach
V	800		144	blue
✖	801		359	brown
8	912		209	dk green
4	954		203	green
2	955		206	lt green
◉	956		40	pink
◐	971		316	orange
−	996		433	bright blue
✚	3608		86	fuchsia
Π	3708		31	lt pink
✔	3746		1030	purple
❖	3806		62	rose
▢	Grey area indicates last row of previous section of design.			

Design was stitched on a 19" x 17" piece of White Aida (14 ct) using 3 strands of floss for Cross Stitch and 1 strand for Backstitch. It was made into a pillow.

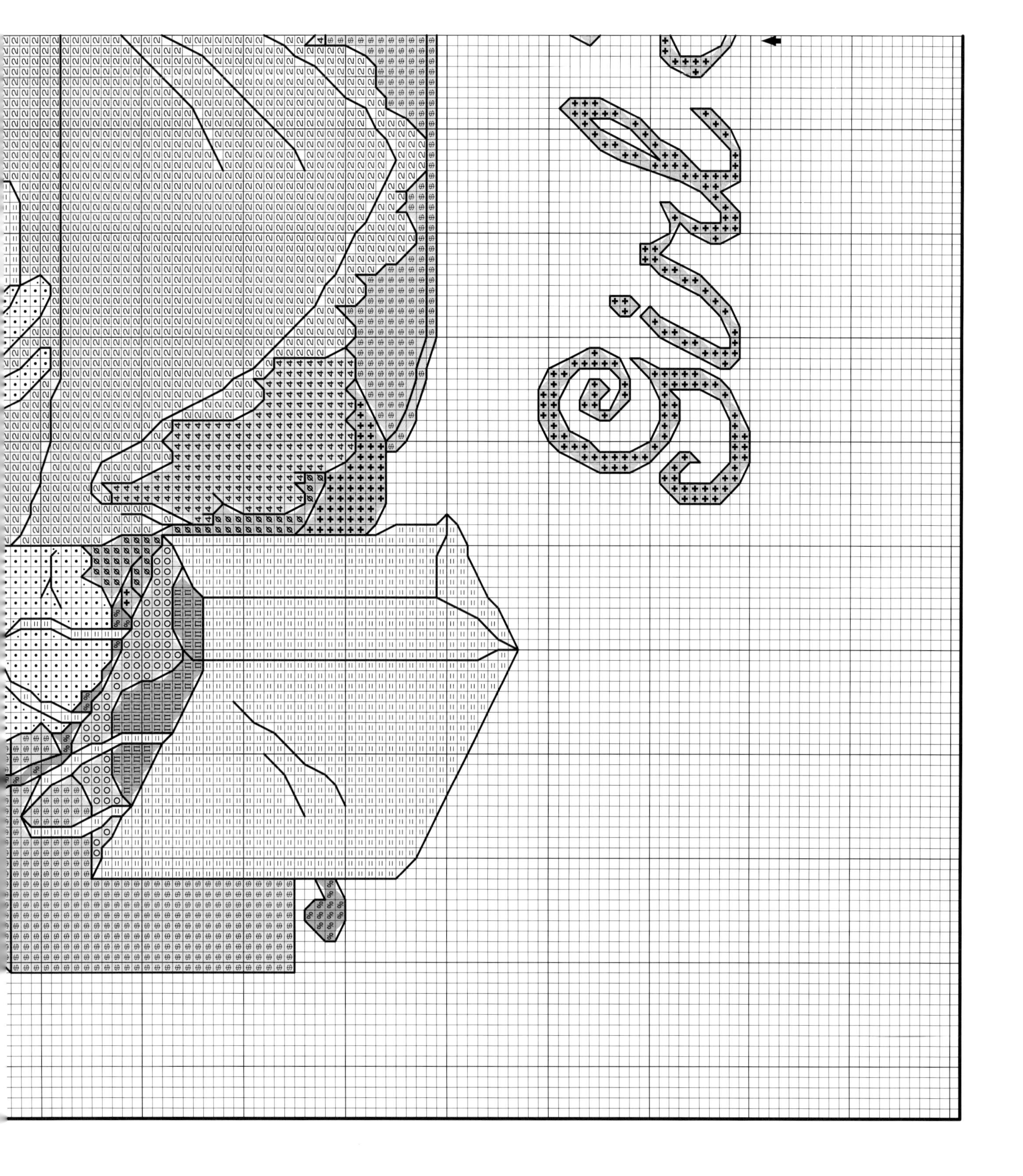

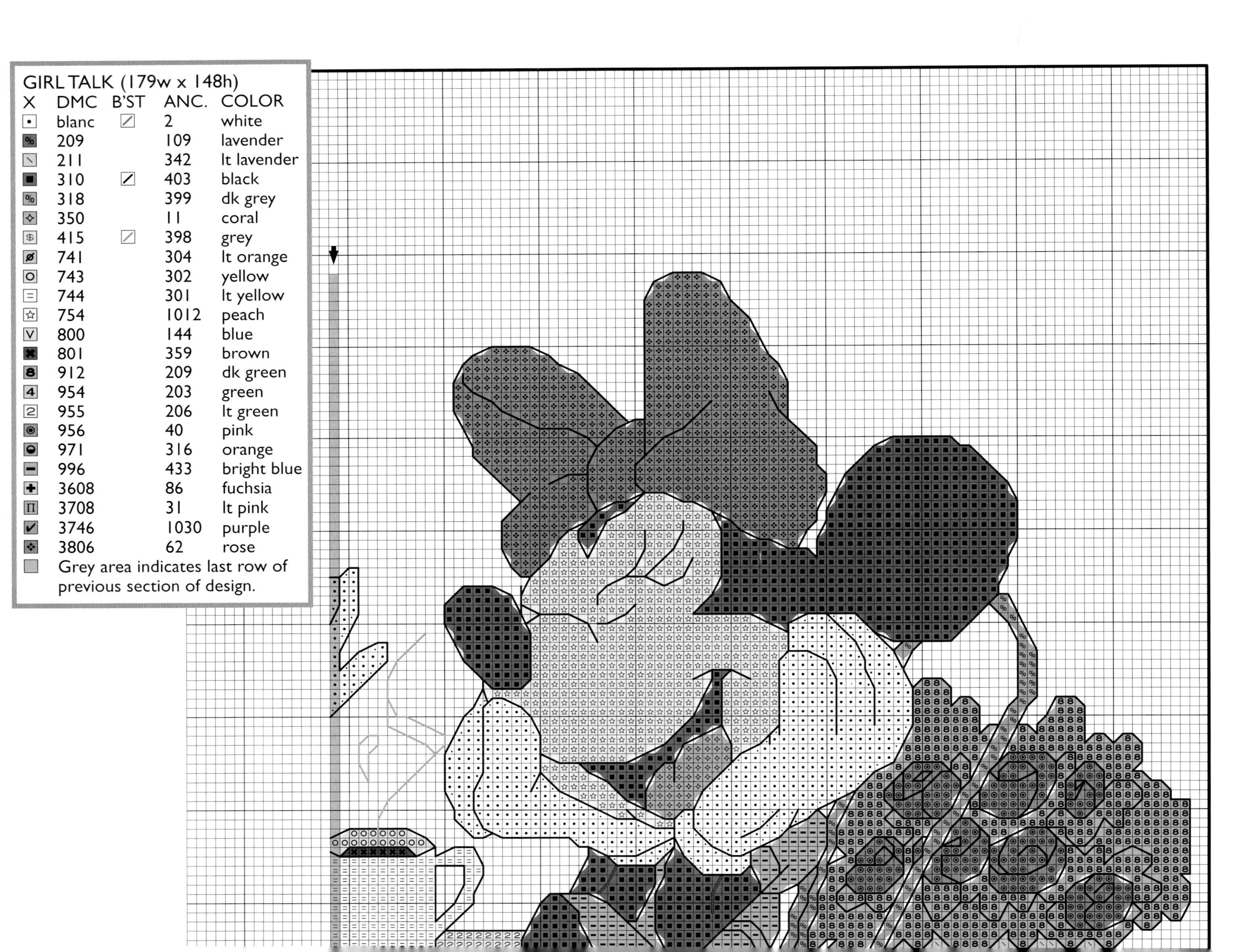
GIRL TALK (179w x 148h)
X DMC B'ST ANC. COLOR
blanc 2 white
209 109 lavender
211 342 lt lavender
310 403 black
318 399 dk grey
350 11 coral
415 398 grey
741 304 lt orange
743 302 yellow
744 301 lt yellow
754 1012 peach
800 144 blue
801 359 brown
912 209 dk green
954 203 green
955 206 lt green
956 40 pink
971 316 orange
996 433 bright blue
3608 86 fuchsia
3708 31 lt pink
3746 1030 purple
3806 62 rose
Grey area indicates last row of previous section of design.

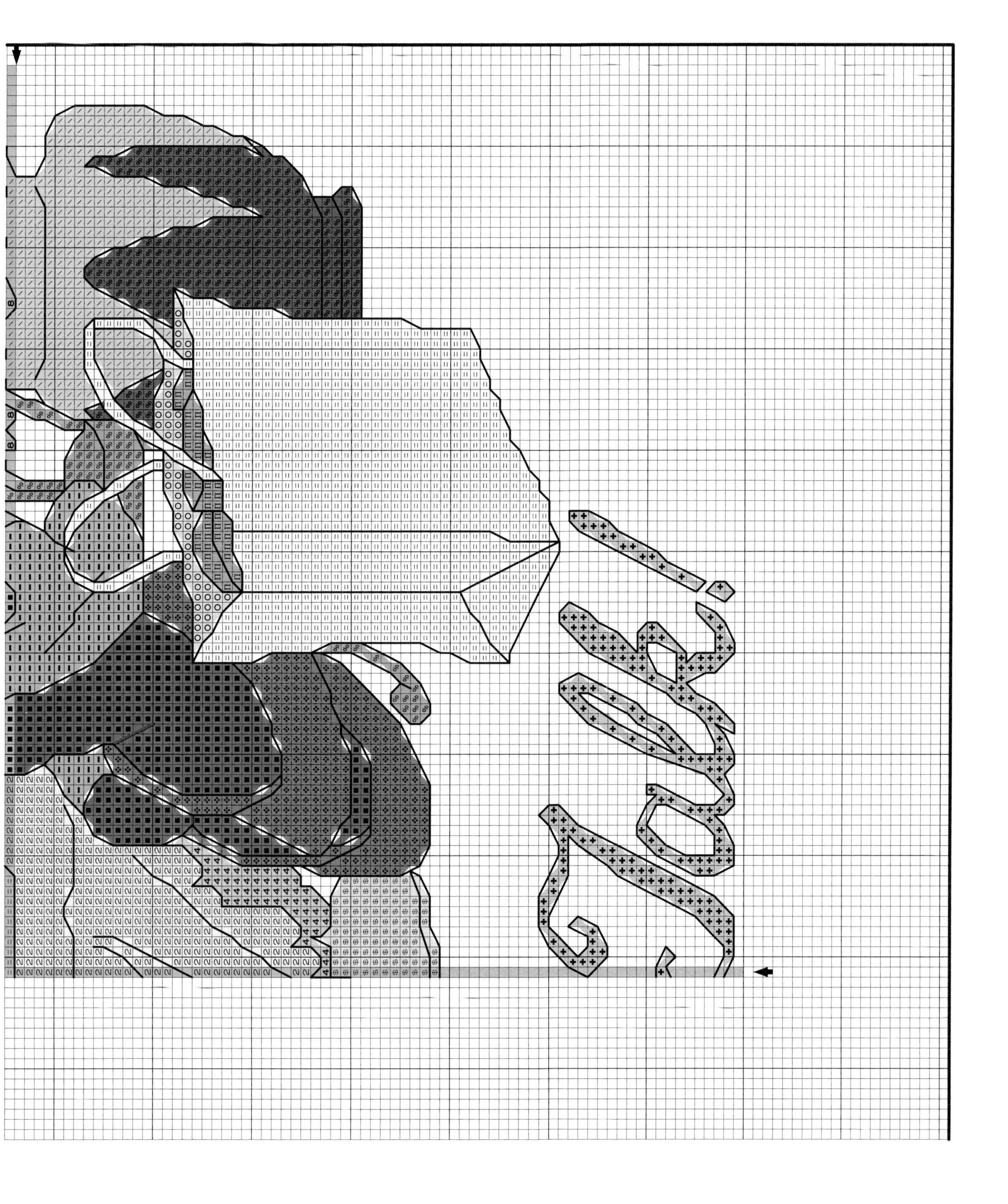

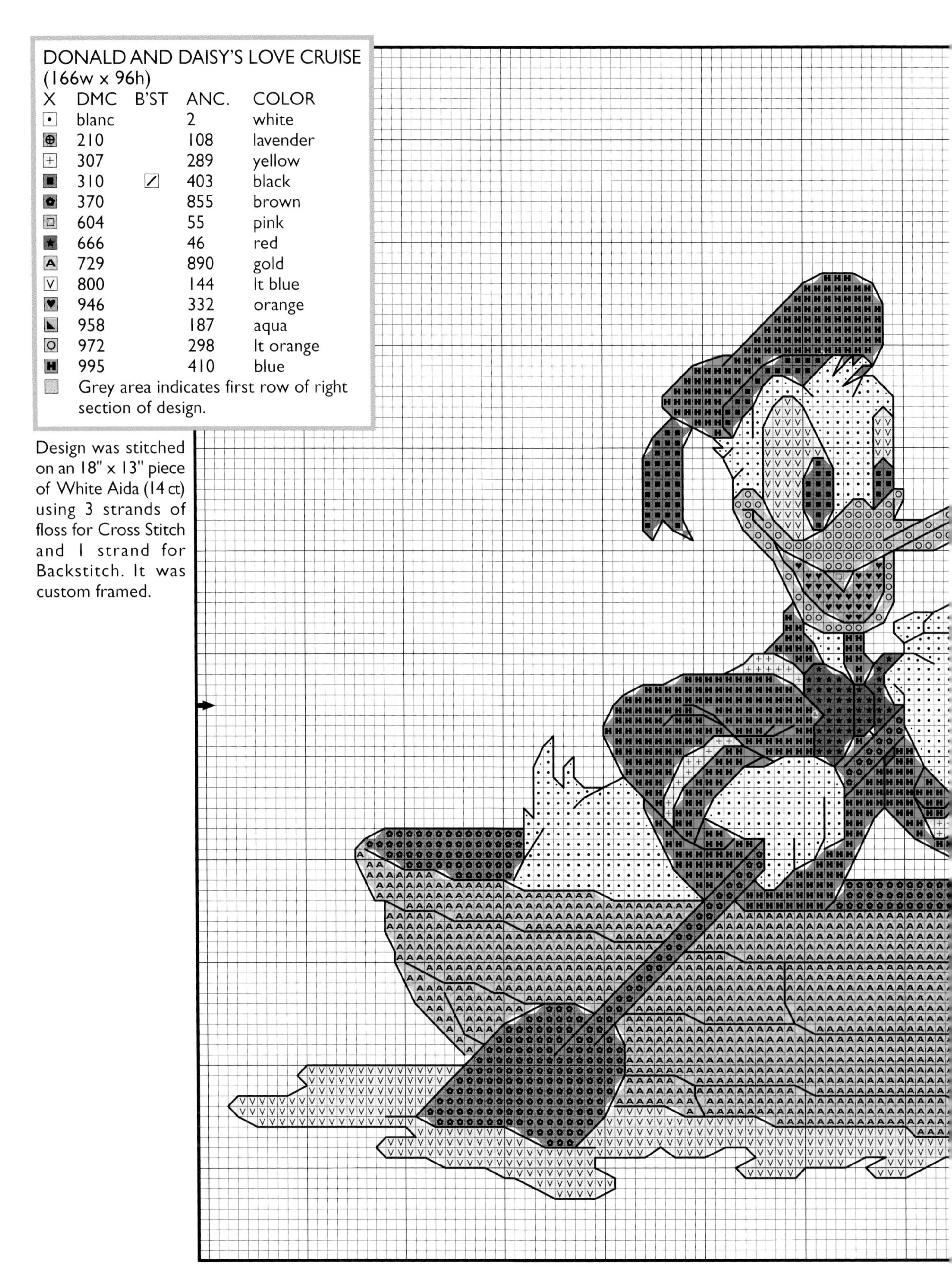

DONALD AND DAISY'S LOVE CRUISE
(166w x 96h)

X	DMC	B'ST	ANC.	COLOR
•	blanc		2	white
⊕	210		108	lavender
+	307		289	yellow
■	310	/	403	black
✿	370		855	brown
□	604		55	pink
★	666		46	red
A	729		890	gold
V	800		144	lt blue
♥	946		332	orange
◣	958		187	aqua
O	972		298	lt orange
H	995		410	blue
	Grey area indicates first row of right section of design.			

Design was stitched on an 18" x 13" piece of White Aida (14 ct) using 3 strands of floss for Cross Stitch and 1 strand for Backstitch. It was custom framed.

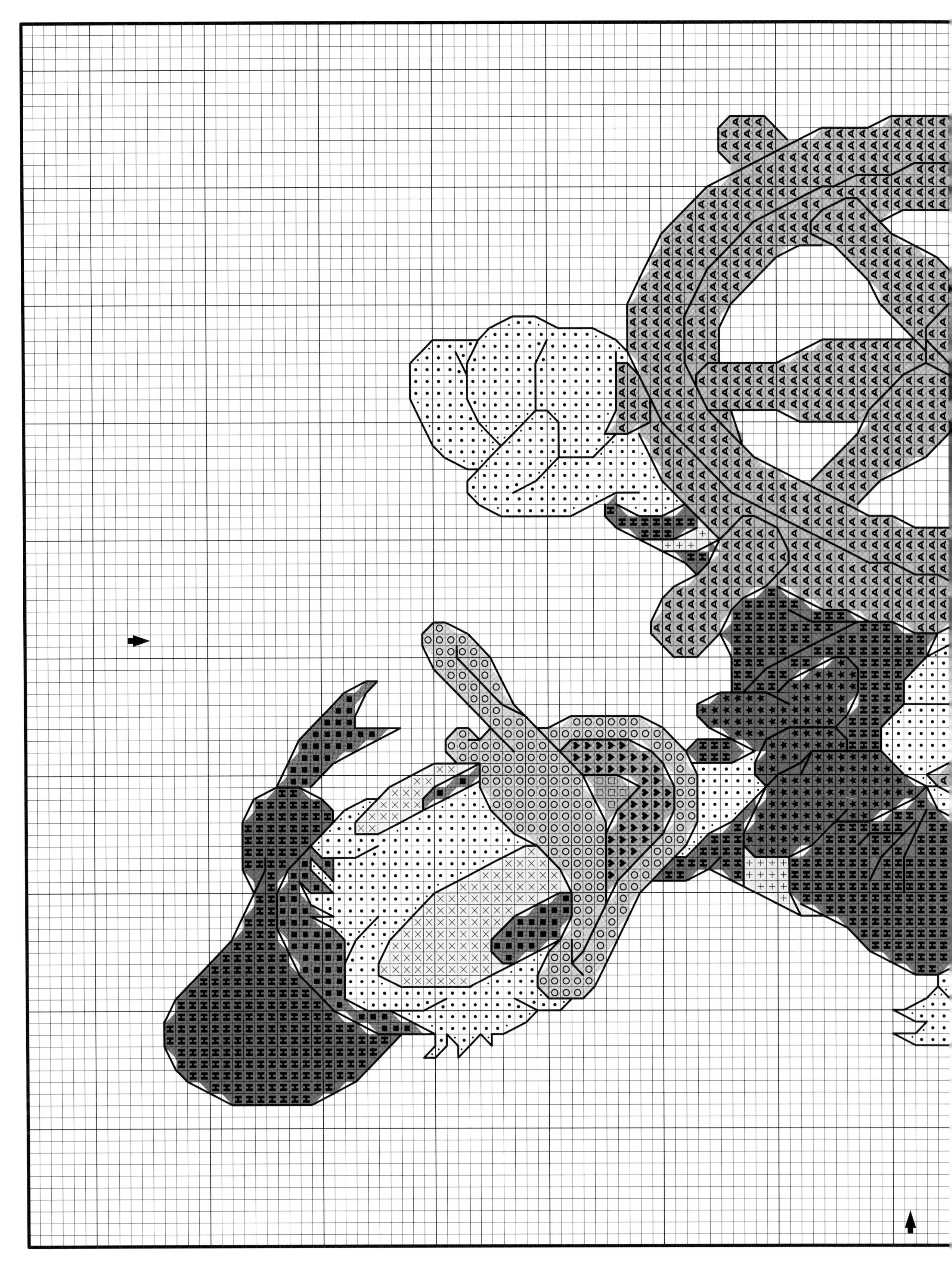

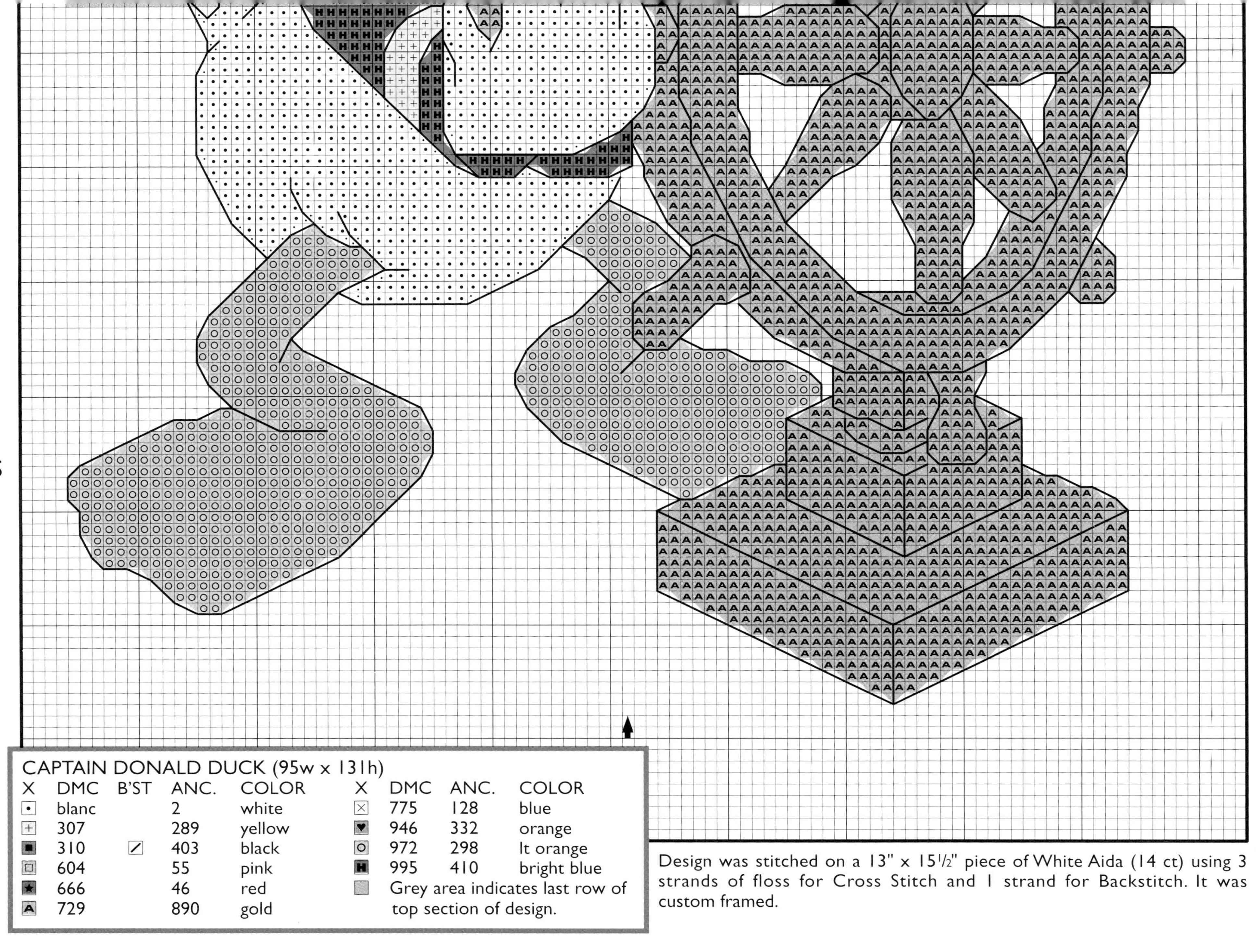

CAPTAIN DONALD DUCK (95w x 131h)

X	DMC	B'ST	ANC.	COLOR
•	blanc		2	white
+	307		289	yellow
■	310	⁄	403	black
□	604		55	pink
★	666		46	red
A	729		890	gold

X	DMC	ANC.	COLOR
☒	775	128	blue
♥	946	332	orange
O	972	298	lt orange
H	995	410	bright blue
░	Grey area indicates last row of top section of design.		

Design was stitched on a 13" x 15½" piece of White Aida (14 ct) using 3 strands of floss for Cross Stitch and 1 strand for Backstitch. It was custom framed.

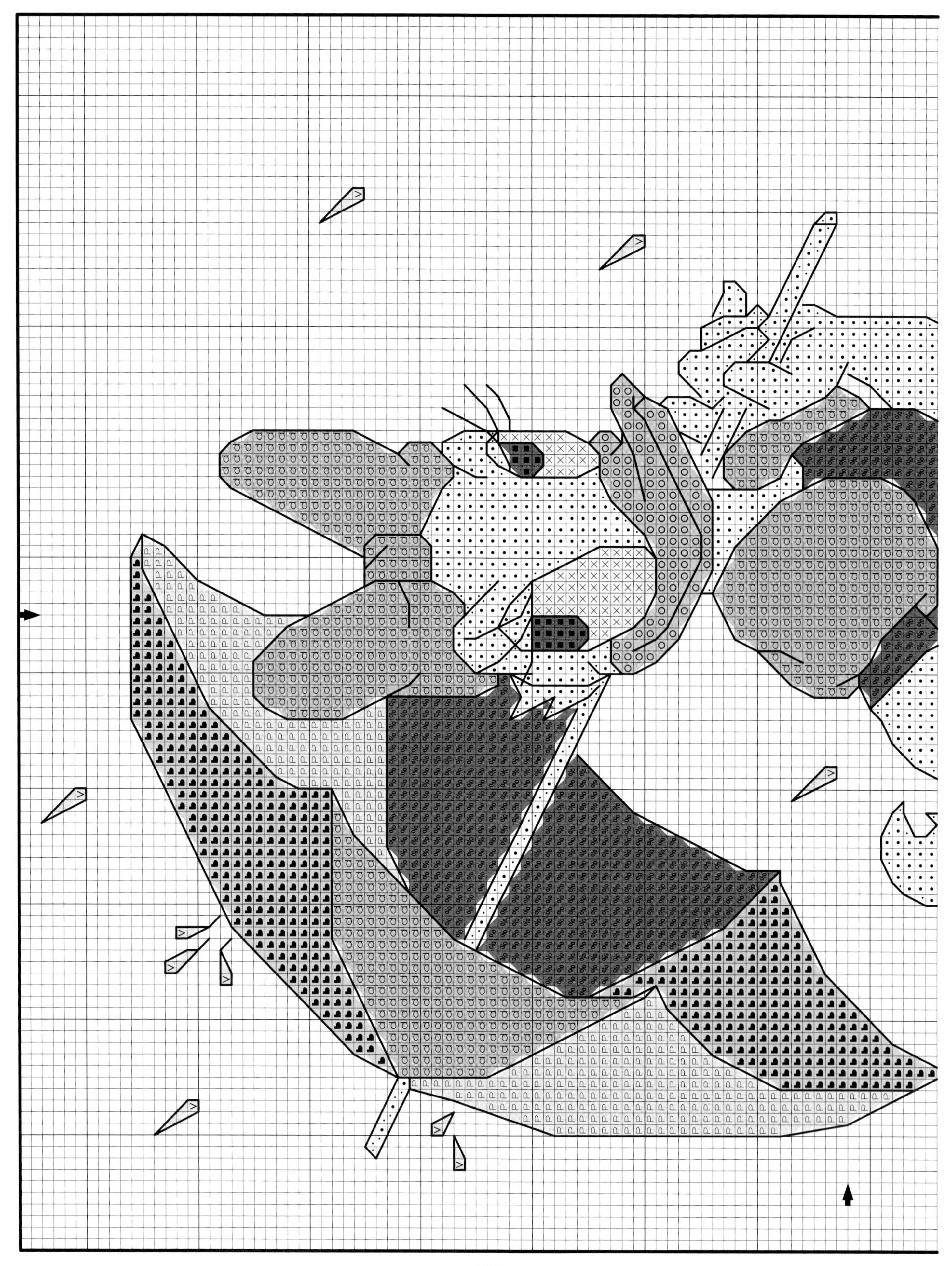

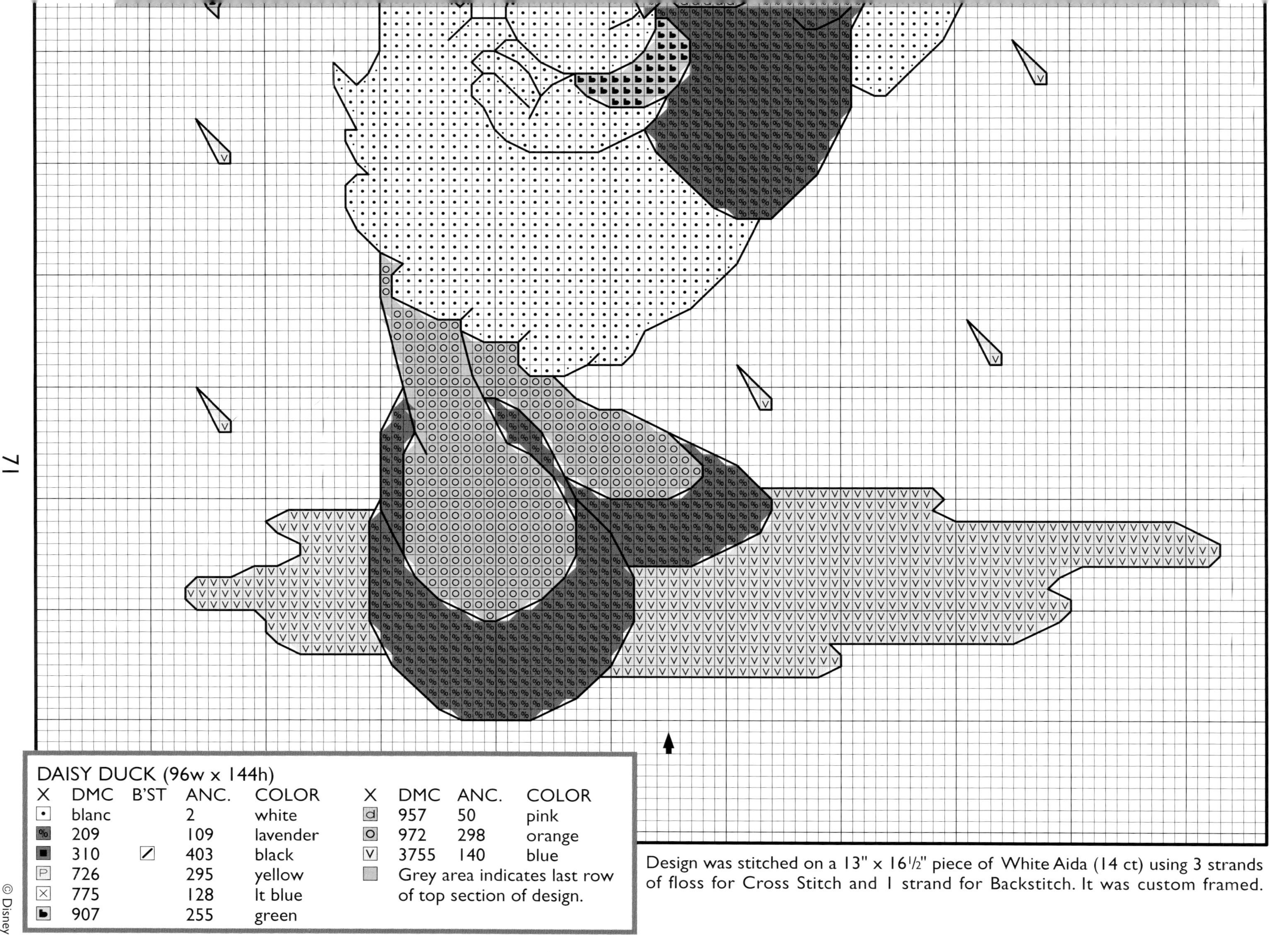

DAISY DUCK (96w x 144h)

X	DMC	B'ST	ANC.	COLOR
•	blanc		2	white
%	209		109	lavender
■	310	/	403	black
P	726		295	yellow
⊠	775		128	lt blue
◣	907		255	green

X	DMC	ANC.	COLOR
d	957	50	pink
O	972	298	orange
V	3755	140	blue
▒	Grey area indicates last row of top section of design.		

Design was stitched on a 13" x 16½" piece of White Aida (14 ct) using 3 strands of floss for Cross Stitch and 1 strand for Backstitch. It was custom framed.

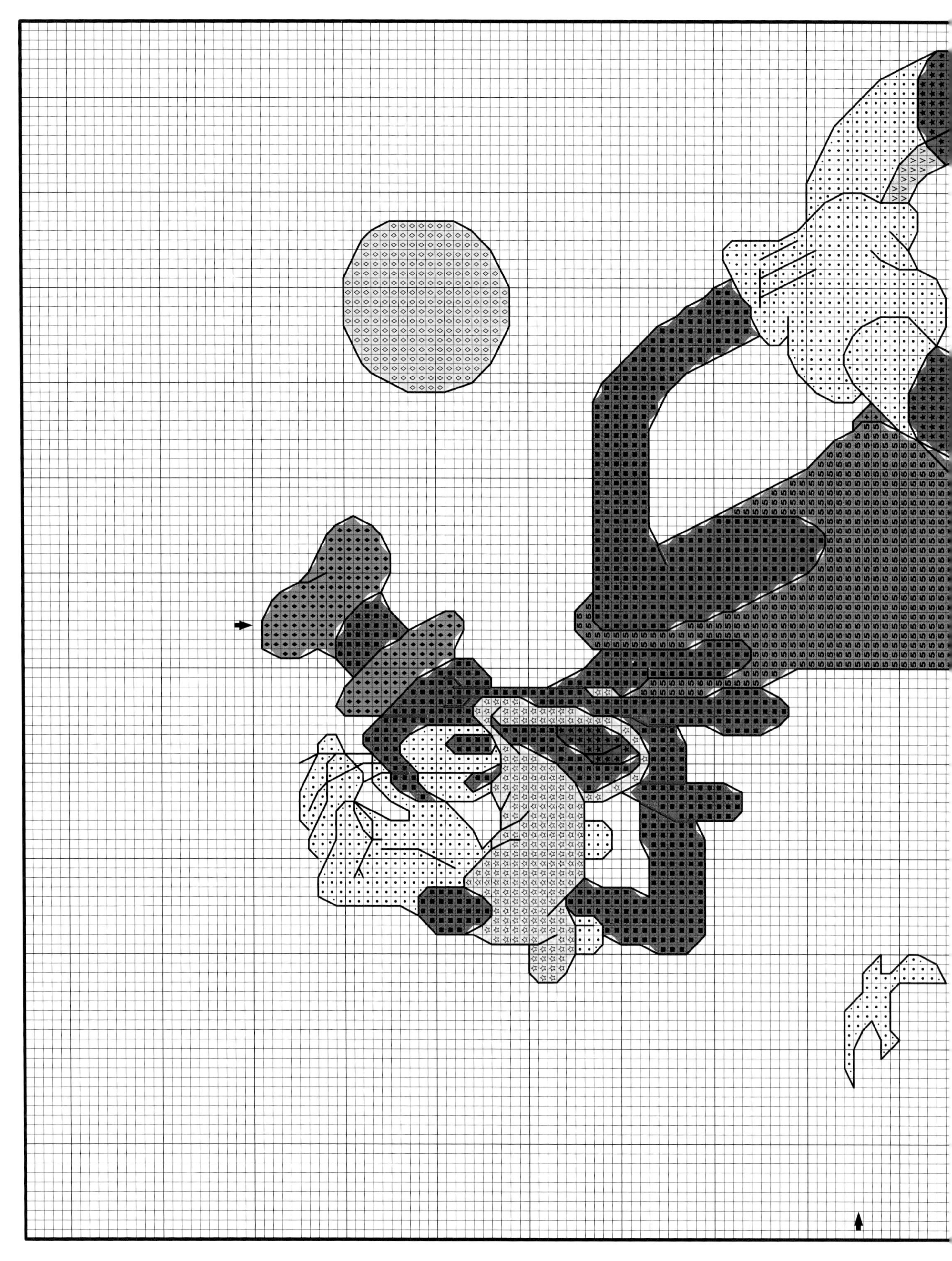

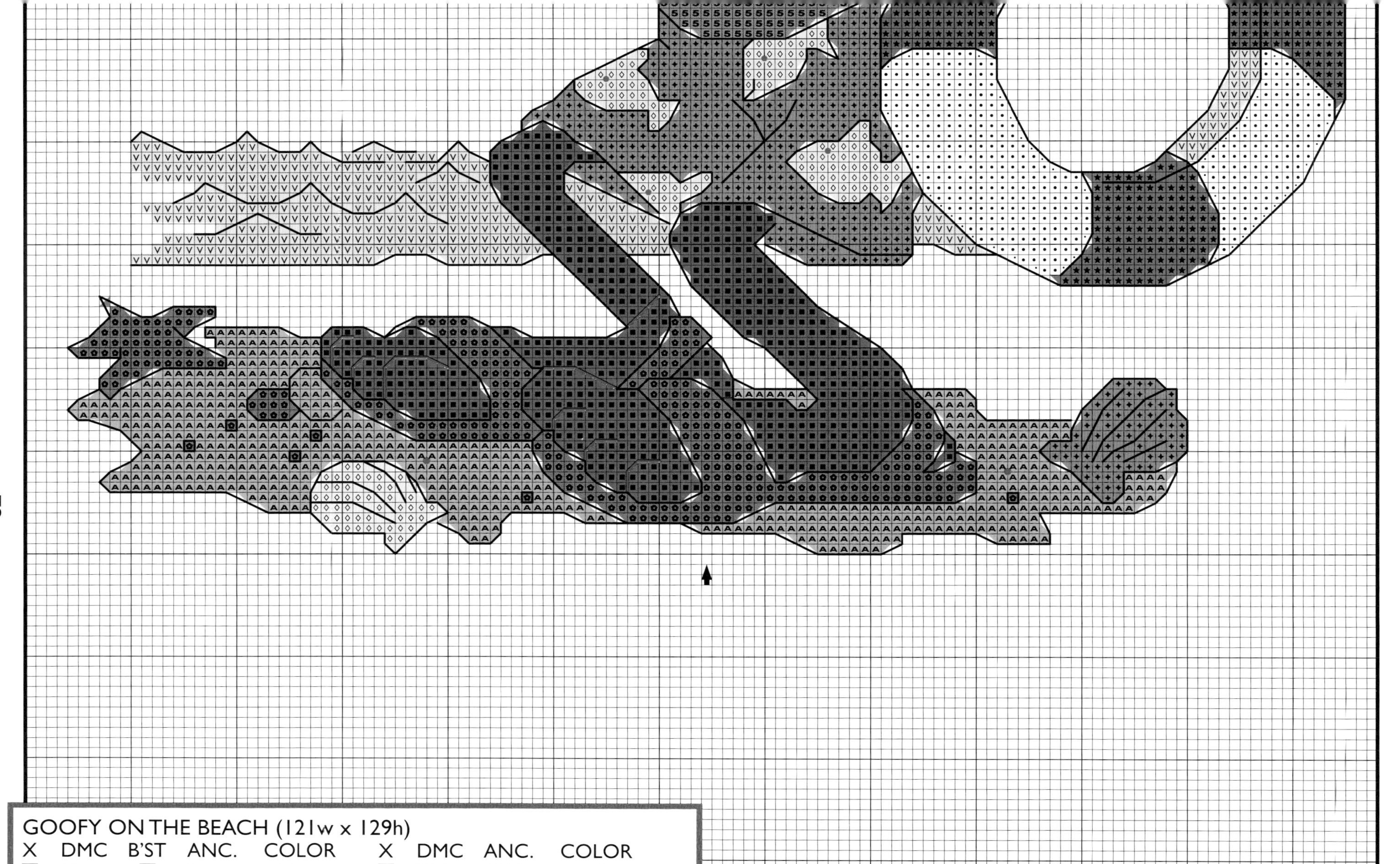

GOOFY ON THE BEACH (121w x 129h)

X	DMC	B'ST	ANC.	COLOR
•	blanc	⁄	2	white
■	310	⁄	403	black
✿	370		855	brown
✦	602		63	pink
★	666		46	red
◆	704		256	green
A	729		890	gold

X	DMC	ANC.	COLOR
☆	754	1012	peach
V	800	144	blue
5	806	169	turquoise
◇	973	297	yellow
•	310	403	black Fr. Knot

Grey area indicates last row of top section of design.

Design was stitched on a 15" x 15½" piece of White Aida (14 ct) using 3 strands of floss for Cross Stitch and 1 strand for Backstitch and French Knots. It was made into a tote bag.

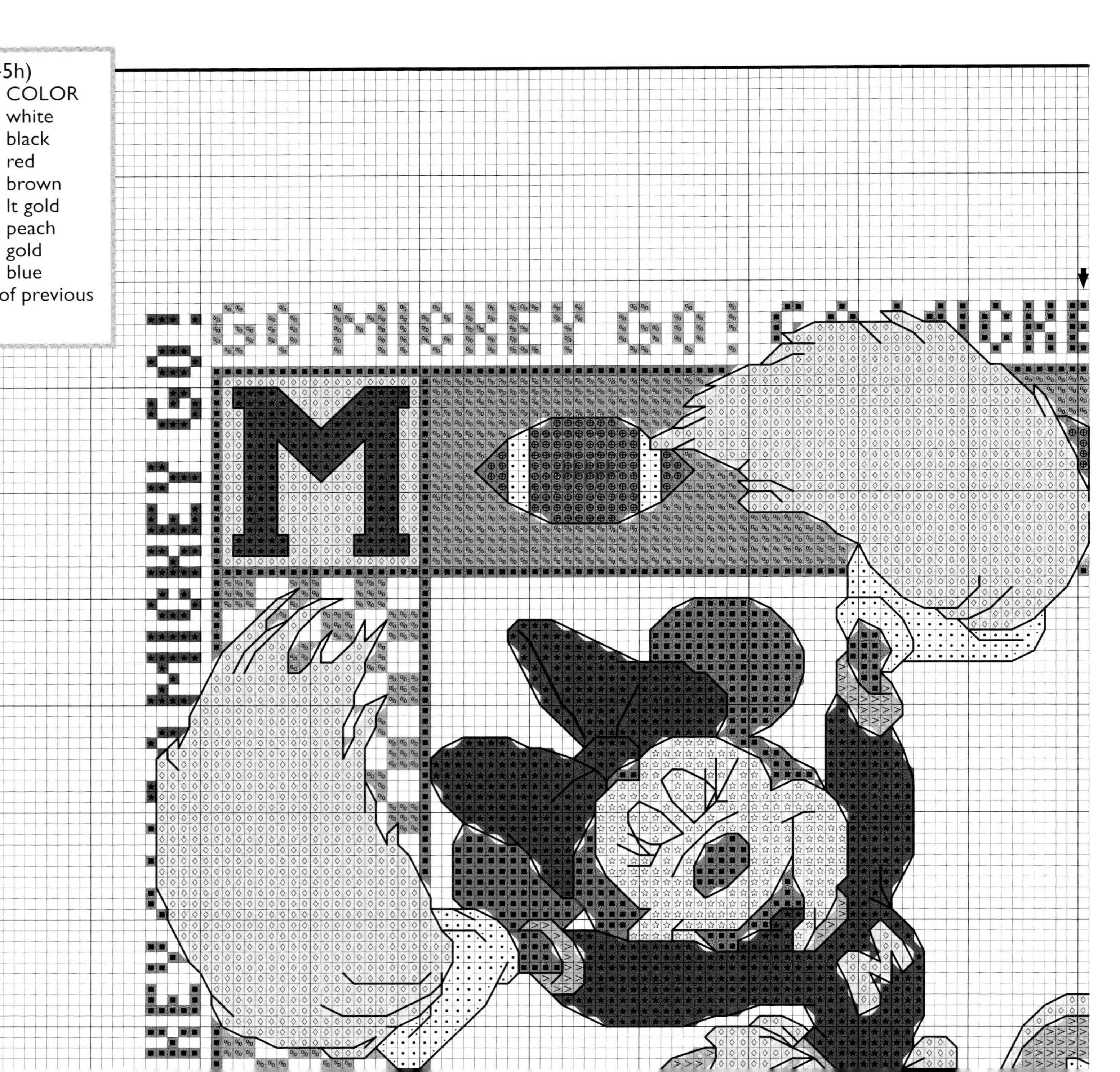

GO MICKEY GO! (171w x 145h)

X	DMC	1/2X	B'ST	ANC.	COLOR
•	blanc		/	2	white
■	310		/	403	black
★	321			9046	red
⊕	434			310	brown
◇	676			891	lt gold
☆	754			1012	peach
>	783			307	gold
%	799	✿		136	blue

Grey area indicates last row of previous section of design.

Design was stitched on an 18½" x 16½" piece of White Aida (14 ct) using 3 strands of floss for Cross Stitch, 2 strands for Half Cross Stitch, and 1 strand for Backstitch. It was made into a pillow.

GO MICKEY GO! (171w x 145h)

X	DMC	1/2X	B'ST	ANC.	COLOR
•	blanc		/	2	white
■	310		/	403	black
★	321			9046	red
⊕	434			310	brown
◇	676			891	lt gold
☆	754			1012	peach
>	783			307	gold
%	799	✿		136	blue

Grey area indicates last row of previous section of design.

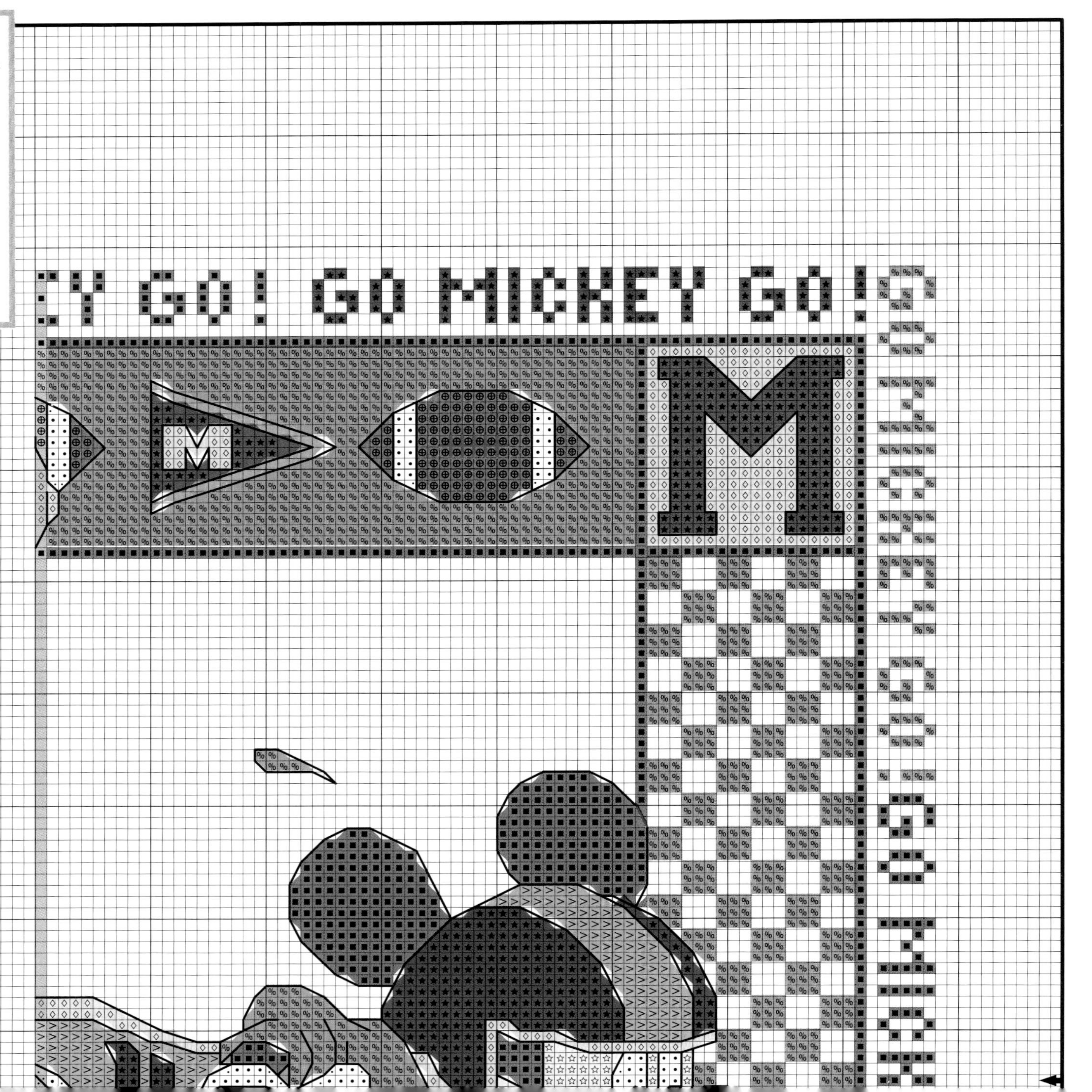

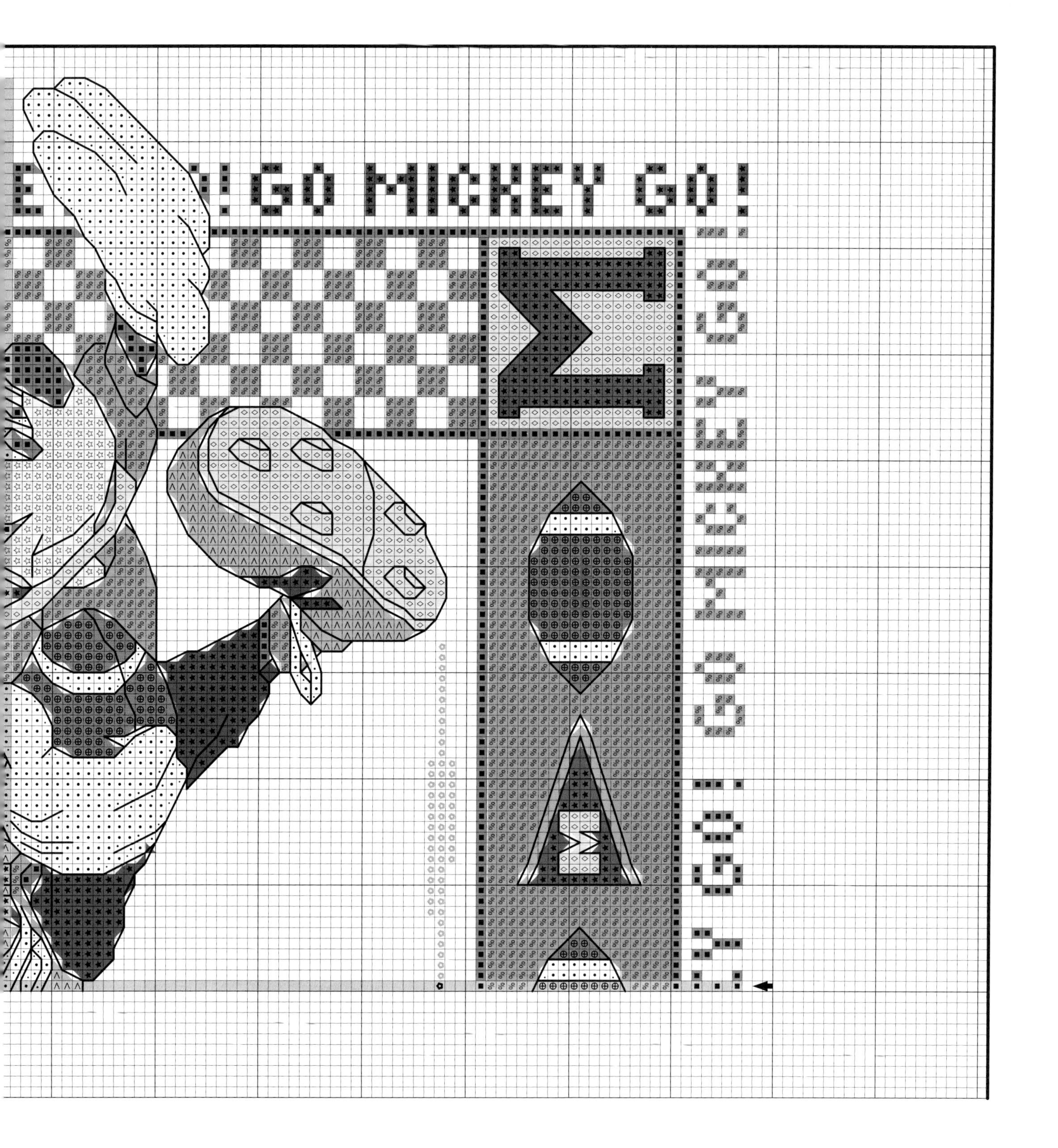
GO MICKEY GO!

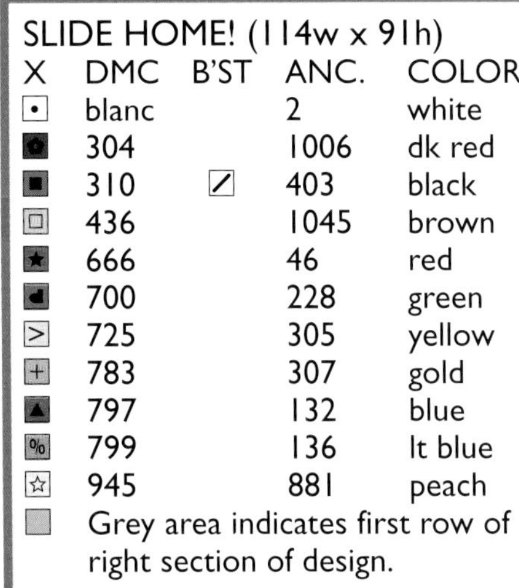

SLIDE HOME! (114w x 91h)

X	DMC	B'ST	ANC.	COLOR
•	blanc		2	white
⬟	304		1006	dk red
■	310	⁄	403	black
□	436		1045	brown
★	666		46	red
◖	700		228	green
>	725		305	yellow
+	783		307	gold
▲	797		132	blue
%	799		136	lt blue
☆	945		881	peach

Grey area indicates first row of right section of design.

Design was stitched on a 14½" x 12½" piece of White Aida (14 ct) using 3 strands of floss for Cross Stitch and 1 strand for Backstitch. It was custom framed.

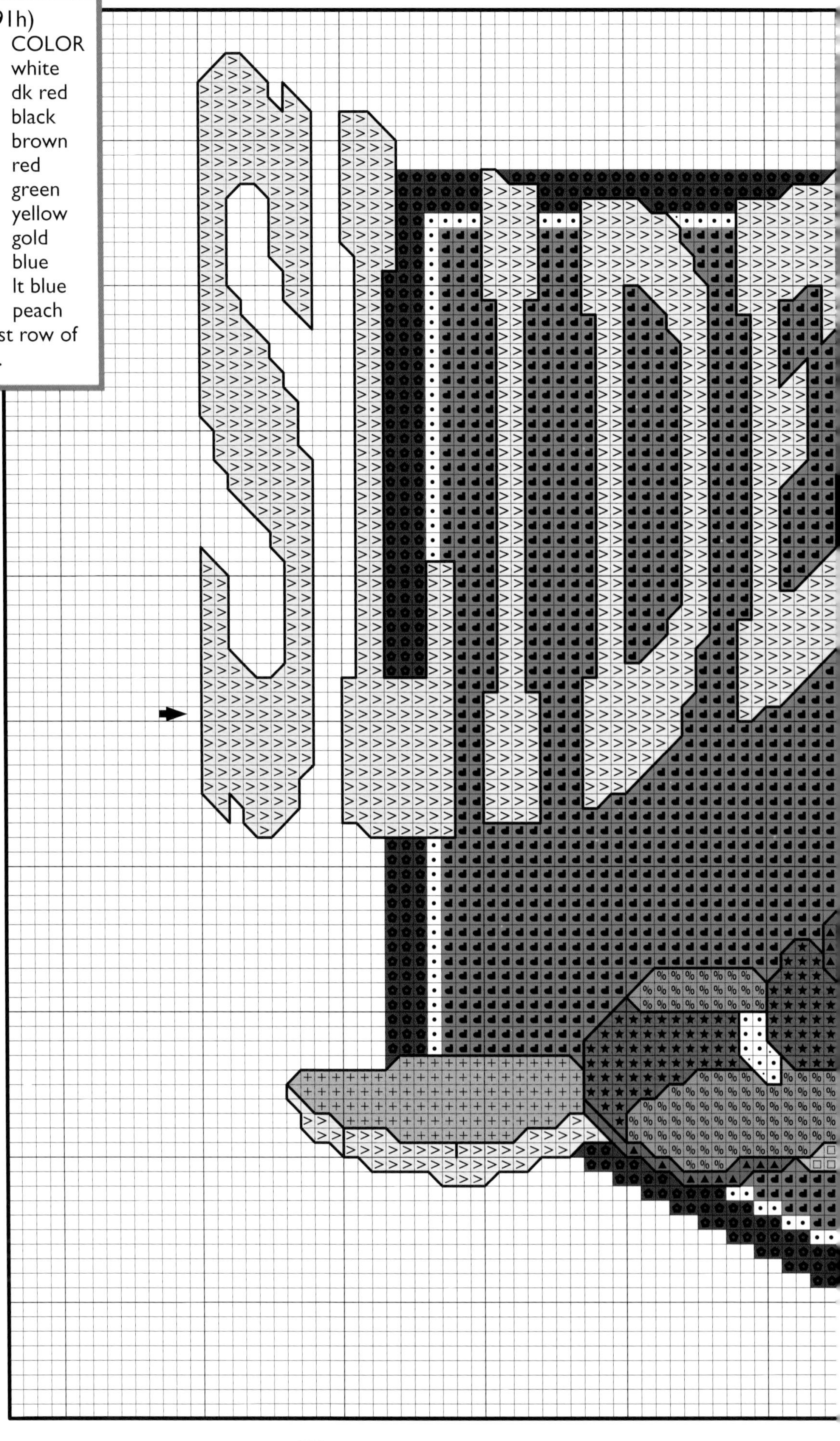

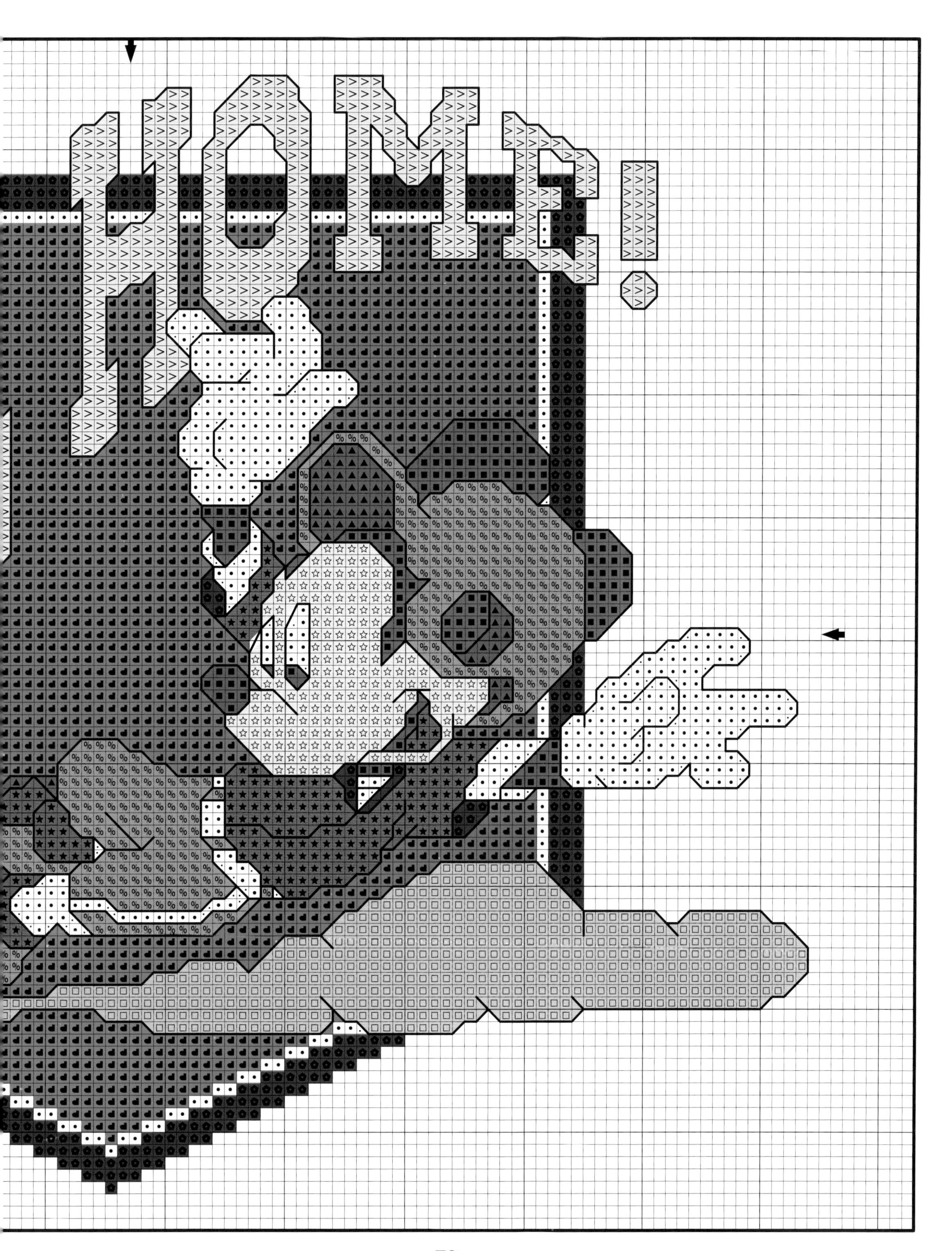

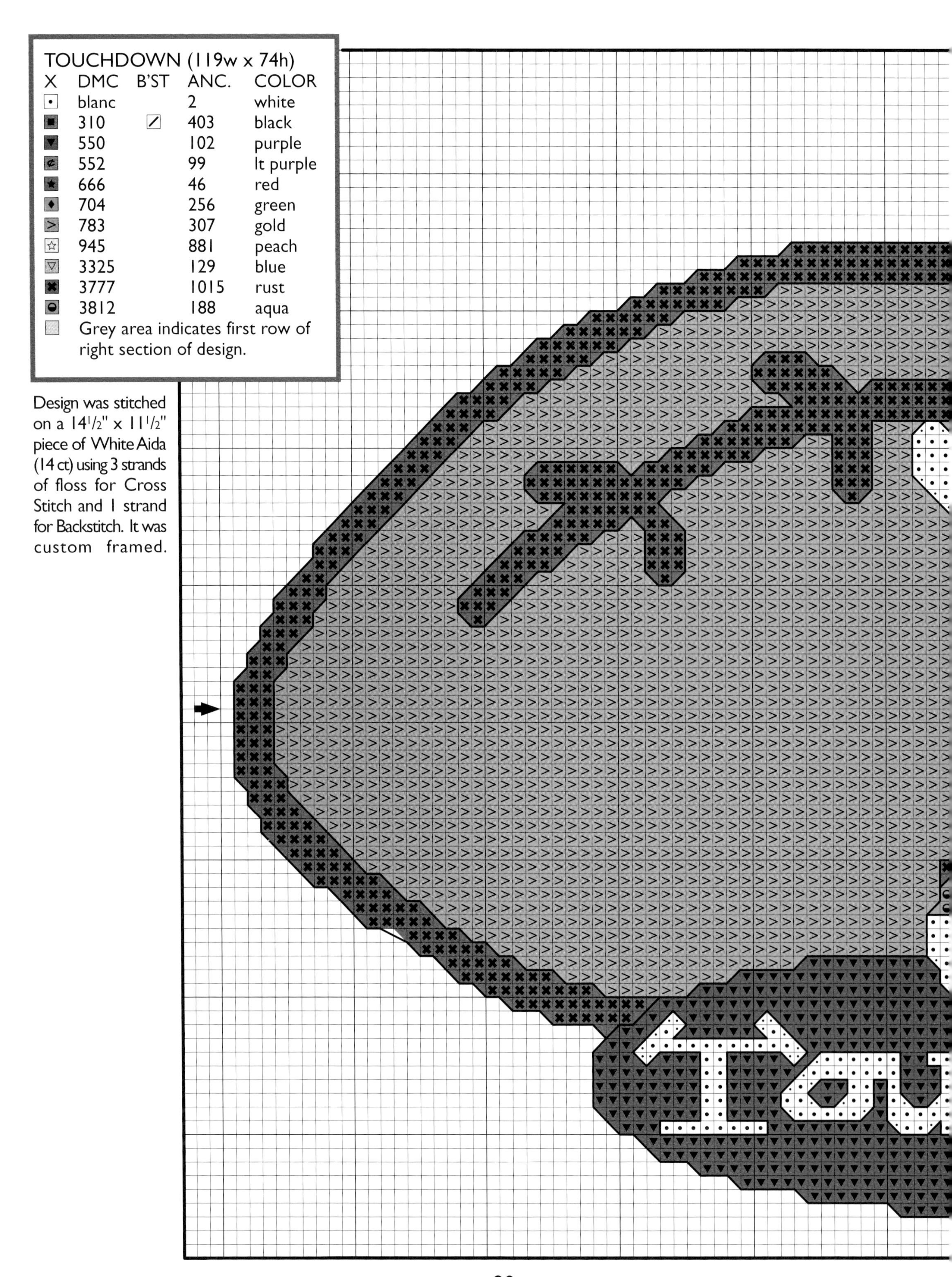

TOUCHDOWN (119w x 74h)

X	DMC	B'ST	ANC.	COLOR
•	blanc		2	white
■	310	⁄	403	black
▼	550		102	purple
¢	552		99	lt purple
★	666		46	red
♦	704		256	green
>	783		307	gold
☆	945		881	peach
▽	3325		129	blue
✖	3777		1015	rust
◒	3812		188	aqua
▢	Grey area indicates first row of right section of design.			

Design was stitched on a 14½" x 11½" piece of White Aida (14 ct) using 3 strands of floss for Cross Stitch and 1 strand for Backstitch. It was custom framed.

chdown

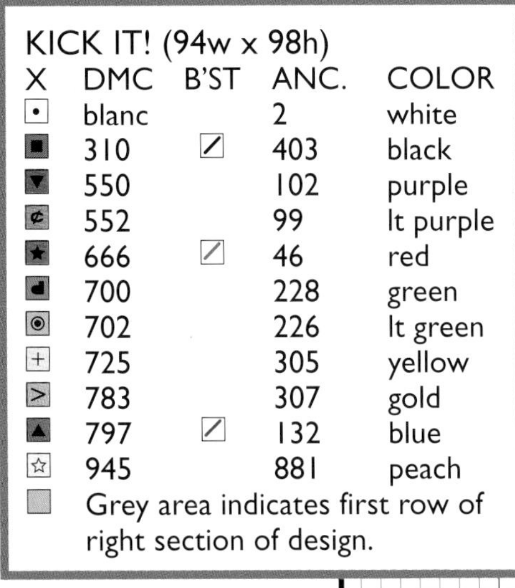

KICK IT! (94w x 98h)

X	DMC	B'ST	ANC.	COLOR
•	blanc		2	white
■	310	/	403	black
▼	550		102	purple
¢	552		99	lt purple
★	666	/	46	red
◖	700		228	green
◎	702		226	lt green
+	725		305	yellow
>	783		307	gold
▲	797	/	132	blue
☆	945		881	peach
░	Grey area indicates first row of right section of design.			

Design was stitched on a 13" x 13" piece of White Aida (14 ct) using 3 strands of floss for Cross Stitch and 1 strand for Backstitch. It was custom framed.

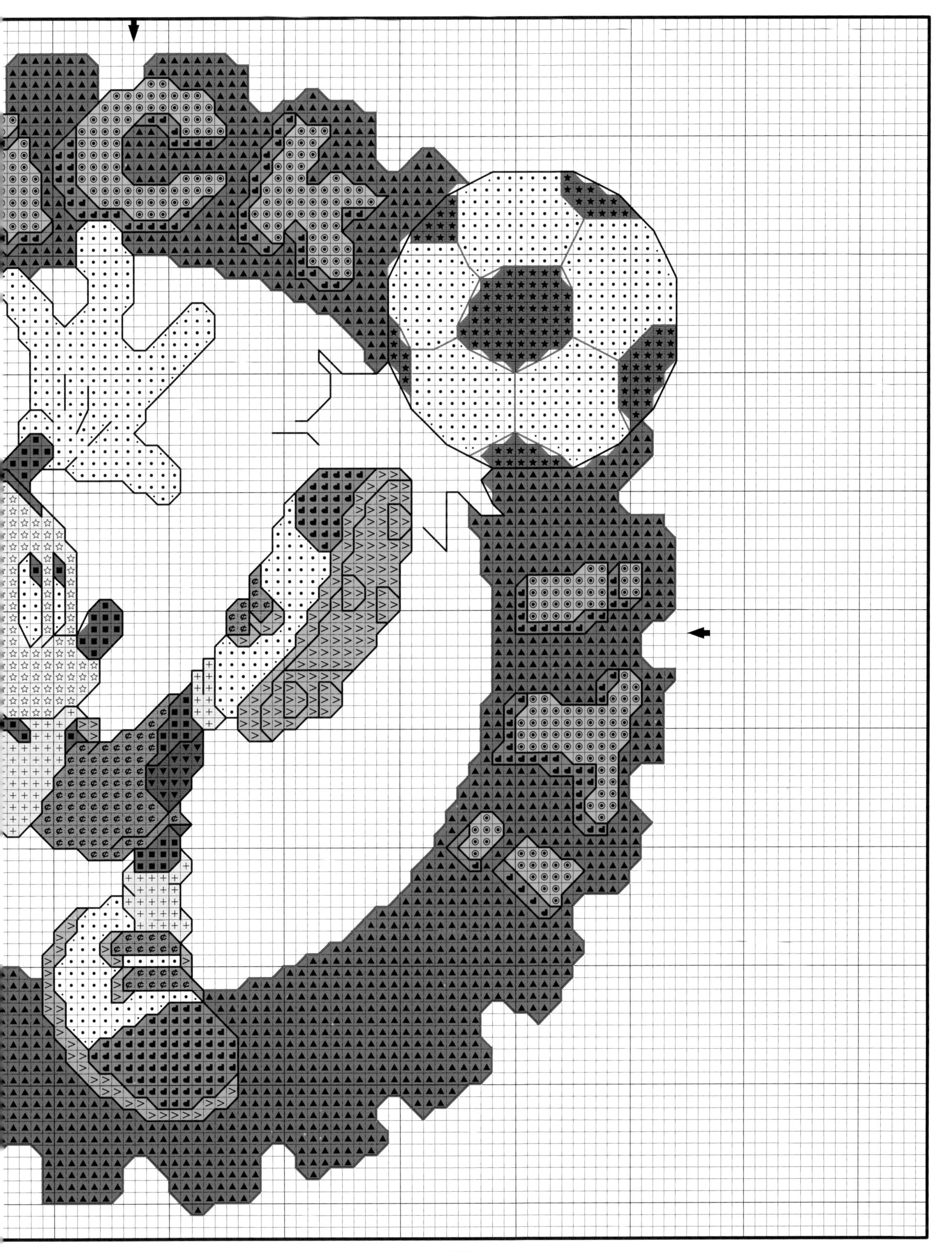

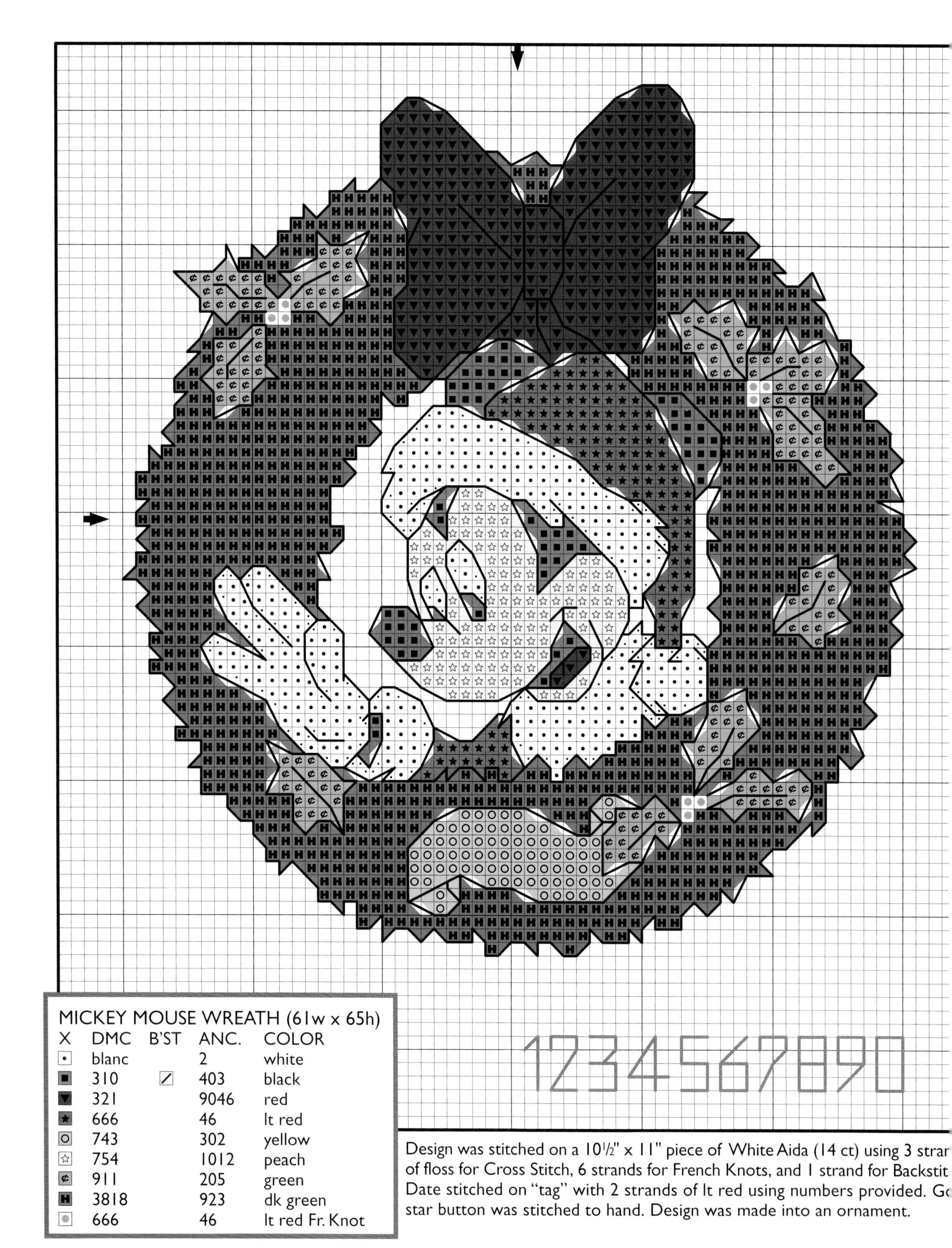

MICKEY MOUSE WREATH (61w x 65h)

X	DMC	B'ST	ANC.	COLOR
•	blanc		2	white
■	310	⁄	403	black
▼	321		9046	red
★	666		46	lt red
O	743		302	yellow
☆	754		1012	peach
¢	911		205	green
H	3818		923	dk green
●	666		46	lt red Fr. Knot

Design was stitched on a 10½" x 11" piece of White Aida (14 ct) using 3 strar of floss for Cross Stitch, 6 strands for French Knots, and 1 strand for Backstit Date stitched on "tag" with 2 strands of lt red using numbers provided. Gc star button was stitched to hand. Design was made into an ornament.

MINNIE MOUSE WREATH (61w x 65h)

X	DMC	B'ST	ANC.	COLOR
•	blanc		2	white
■	310	⁄	403	black
▼	321		9046	red
★	666		46	lt red
○	743		302	yellow
☆	754		1012	peach
¢	911		205	green
H	3818		923	dk green
●	666		46	lt red Fr. Knot

Design was stitched on a 10½" x 11" piece of White Aida (14 ct) using 3 strands of floss for Cross Stitch, 6 strands for French Knots, and 1 strand for Backstitch. Date stitched on "tag" with 2 strands of lt red using numbers provided. Gold star button was stitched to hands. Design was made into an ornament.

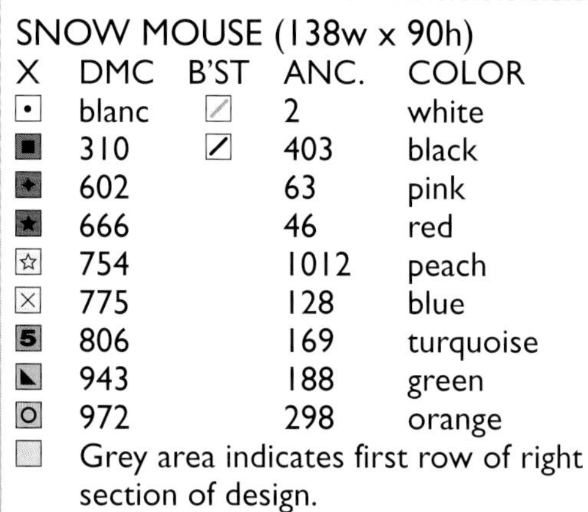

SNOW MOUSE (138w x 90h)

X	DMC	B'ST	ANC.	COLOR
•	blanc	⁄	2	white
■	310	⁄	403	black
◆	602		63	pink
★	666		46	red
☆	754		1012	peach
×	775		128	blue
5	806		169	turquoise
◣	943		188	green
O	972		298	orange
▢	Grey area indicates first row of right section of design.			

Design was stitched on a 16" x 12½" piece of White Aida (14 ct) using 3 strands of floss for Cross Stitch and 1 strand for Backstitch. It was custom framed.

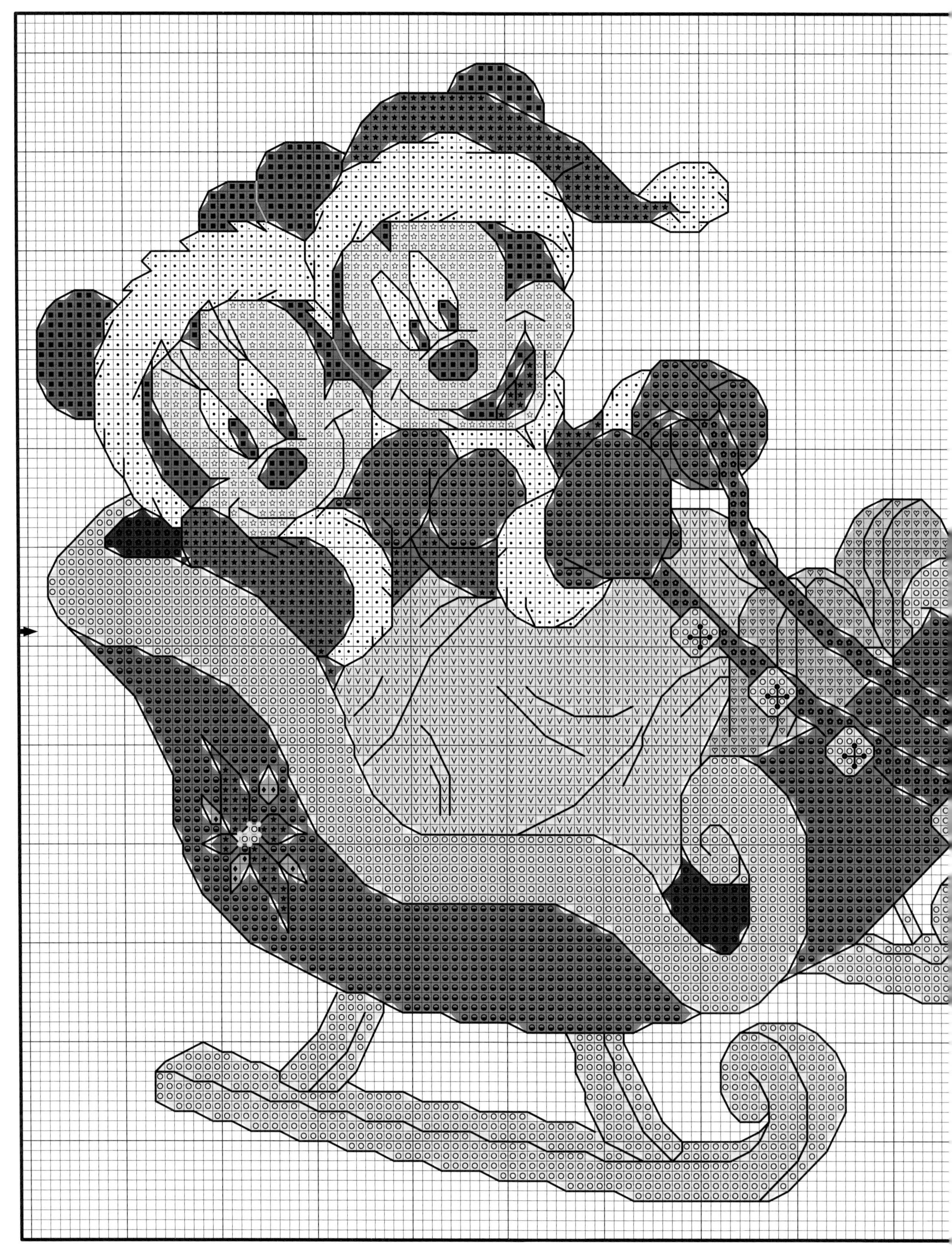

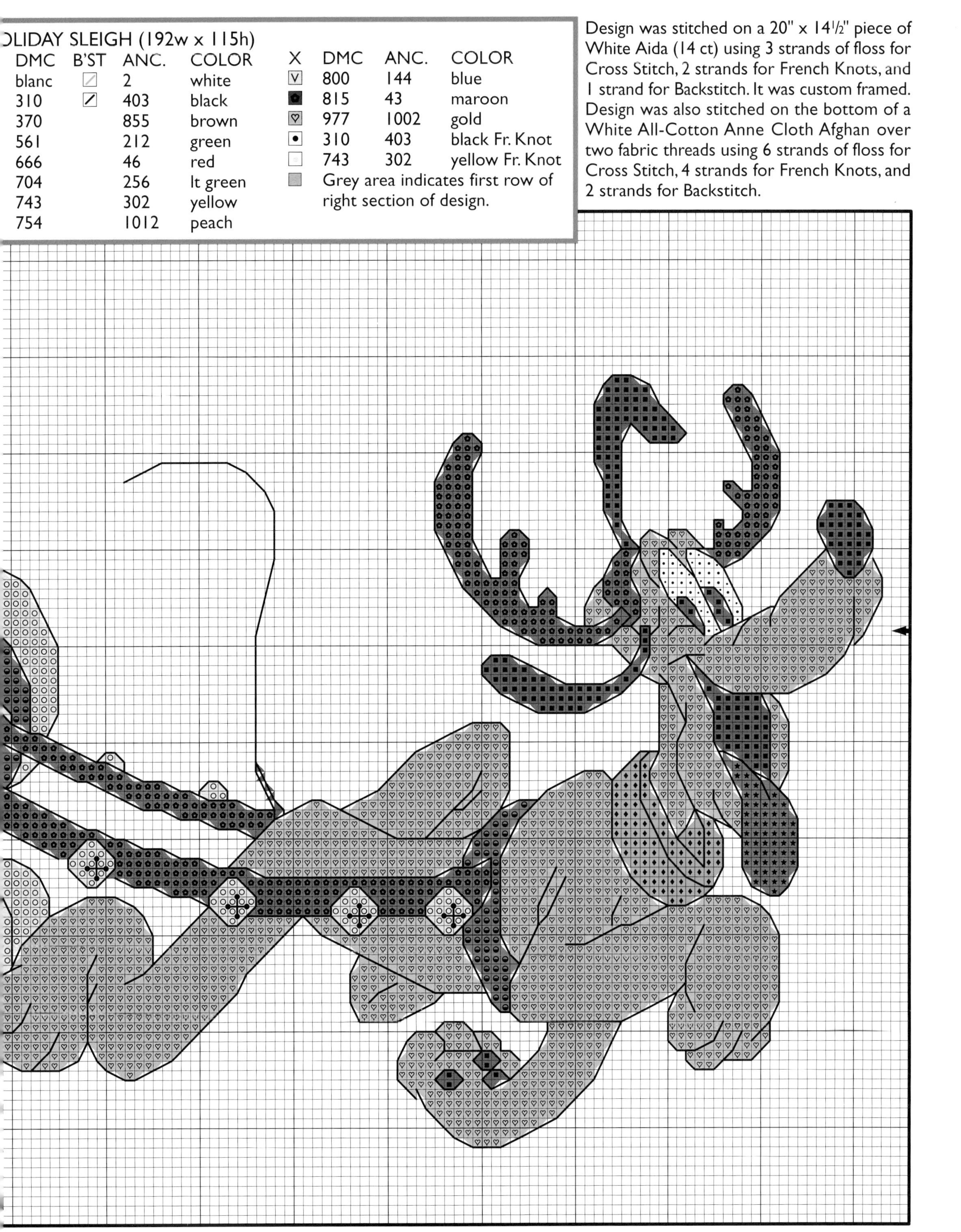

HOLIDAY SLEIGH (192w x 115h)

DMC	B'ST	ANC.	COLOR
blanc	/	2	white
310	/	403	black
370		855	brown
561		212	green
666		46	red
704		256	lt green
743		302	yellow
754		1012	peach

X	DMC	ANC.	COLOR
	800	144	blue
	815	43	maroon
	977	1002	gold
	310	403	black Fr. Knot
	743	302	yellow Fr. Knot
	Grey area indicates first row of right section of design.		

Design was stitched on a 20" x 14½" piece of White Aida (14 ct) using 3 strands of floss for Cross Stitch, 2 strands for French Knots, and 1 strand for Backstitch. It was custom framed. Design was also stitched on the bottom of a White All-Cotton Anne Cloth Afghan over two fabric threads using 6 strands of floss for Cross Stitch, 4 strands for French Knots, and 2 strands for Backstitch.

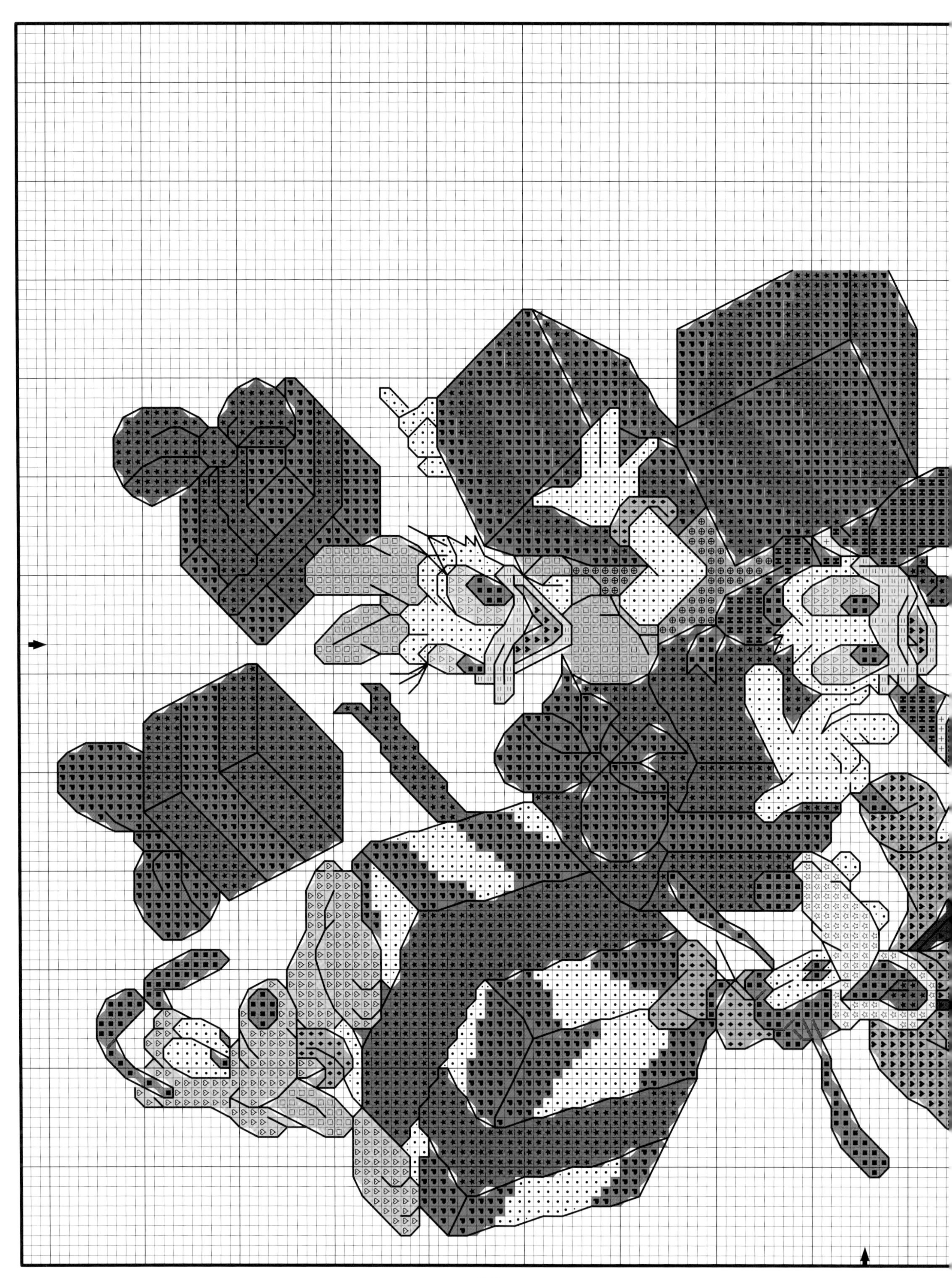

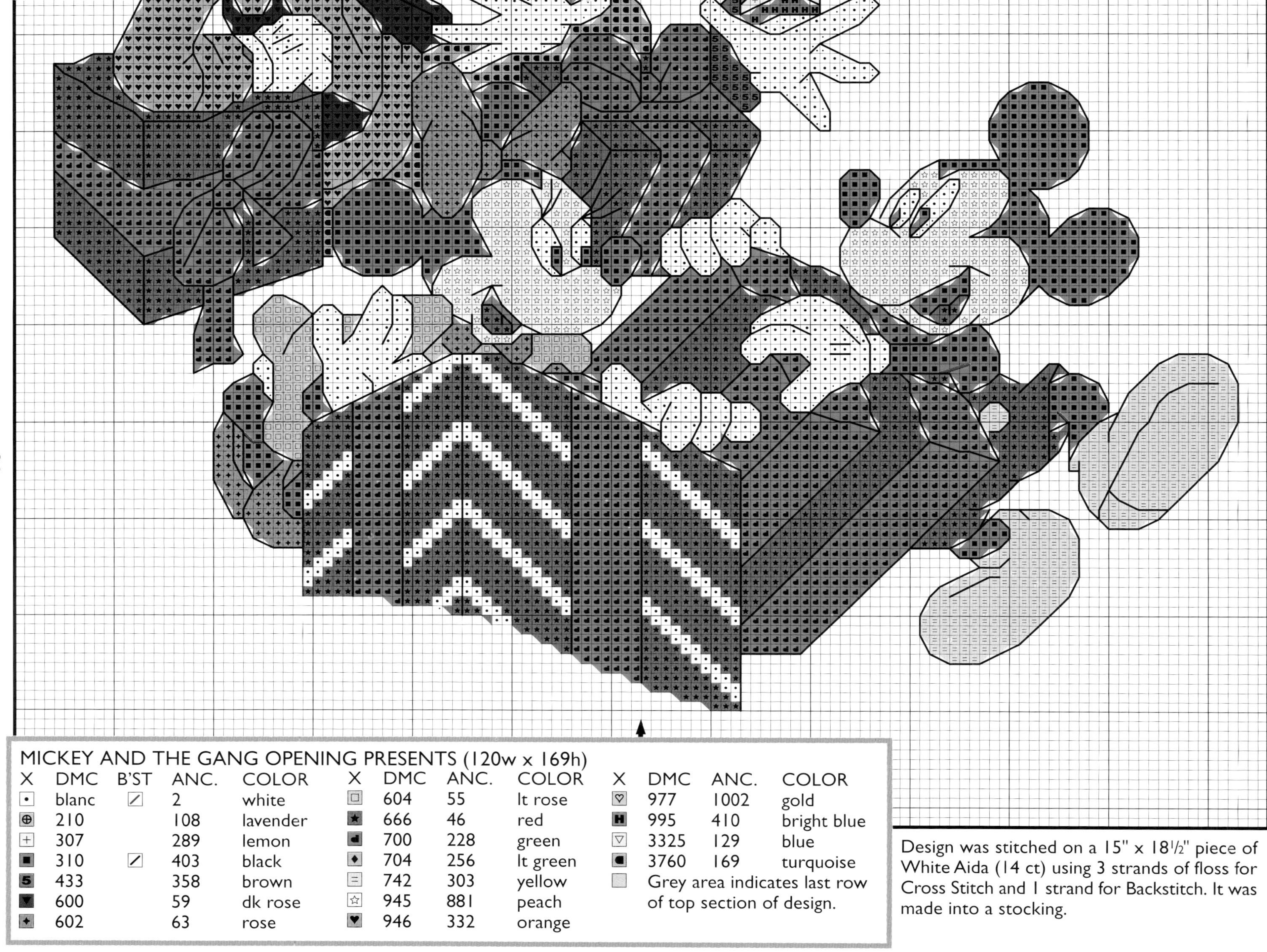

MICKEY AND THE GANG OPENING PRESENTS (120w x 169h)

X	DMC	B'ST	ANC.	COLOR
•	blanc	⁄	2	white
⊕	210		108	lavender
+	307		289	lemon
■	310	⁄	403	black
5	433		358	brown
▼	600		59	dk rose
✦	602		63	rose

X	DMC	ANC.	COLOR
□	604	55	lt rose
★	666	46	red
◘	700	228	green
◆	704	256	lt green
=	742	303	yellow
☆	945	881	peach
♥	946	332	orange

X	DMC	ANC.	COLOR
♡	977	1002	gold
H	995	410	bright blue
▽	3325	129	blue
◖	3760	169	turquoise
▢	Grey area indicates last row of top section of design.		

Design was stitched on a 15" x 18½" piece of White Aida (14 ct) using 3 strands of floss for Cross Stitch and 1 strand for Backstitch. It was made into a stocking.

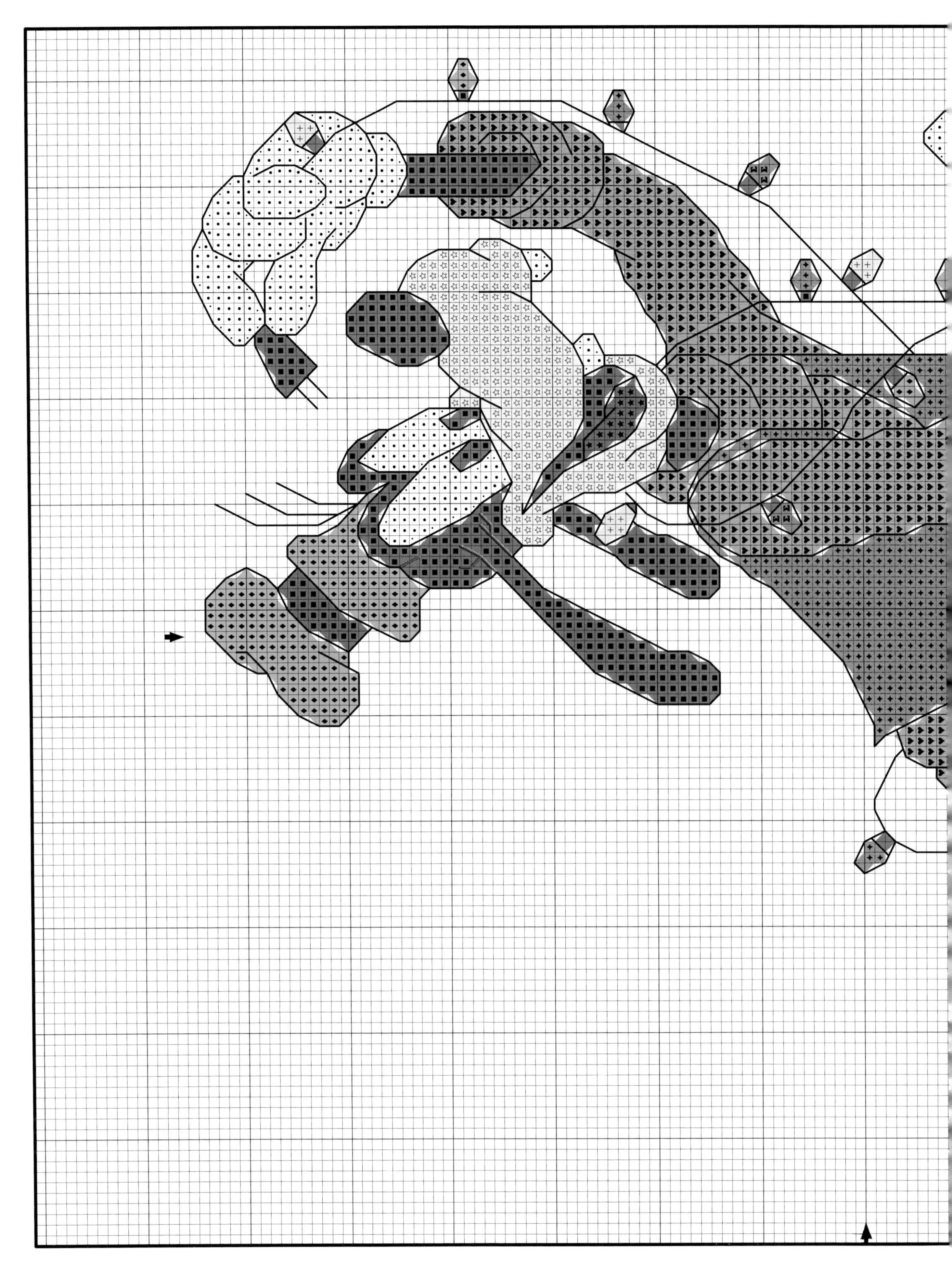

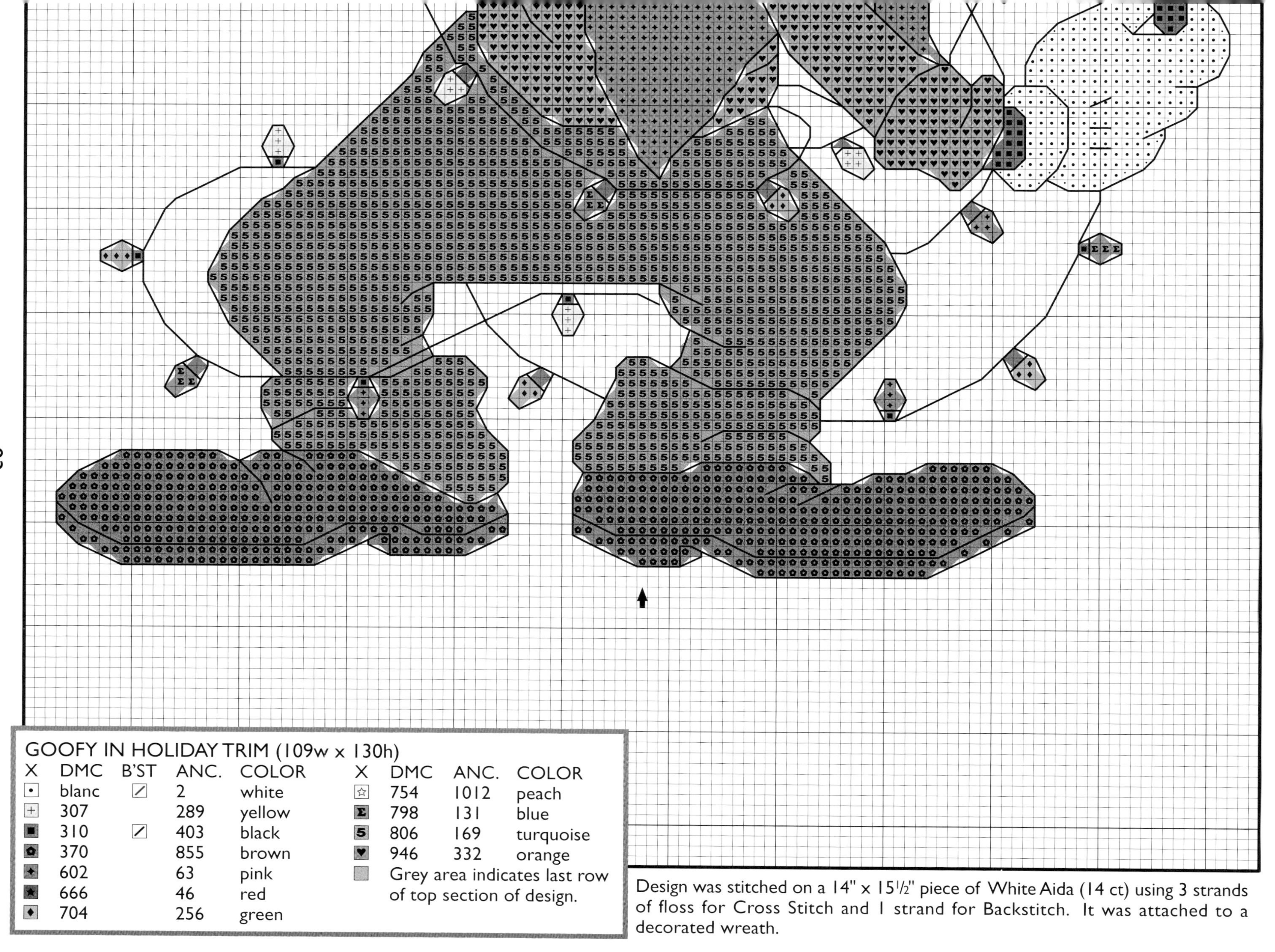

GOOFY IN HOLIDAY TRIM (109w x 130h)

X	DMC	B'ST	ANC.	COLOR
•	blanc	/	2	white
+	307		289	yellow
■	310	/	403	black
✿	370		855	brown
✦	602		63	pink
★	666		46	red
♦	704		256	green

X	DMC	ANC.	COLOR
☆	754	1012	peach
Σ	798	131	blue
5	806	169	turquoise
♥	946	332	orange

Grey area indicates last row of top section of design.

Design was stitched on a 14" x 15½" piece of White Aida (14 ct) using 3 strands of floss for Cross Stitch and 1 strand for Backstitch. It was attached to a decorated wreath.

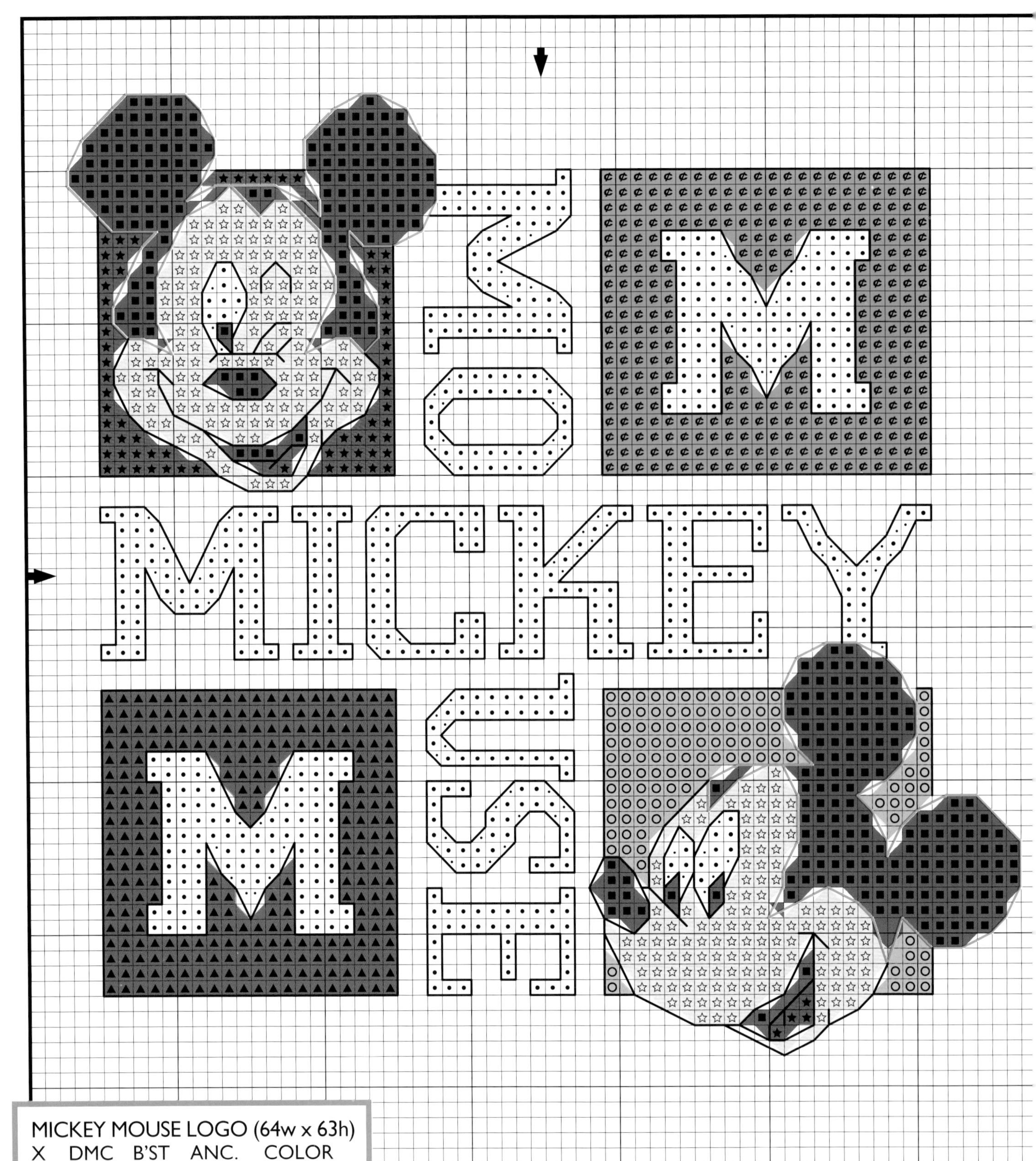

MICKEY MOUSE LOGO (64w x 63h)

X	DMC	B'ST	ANC.	COLOR
•	blanc		2	white
■	310	/	403	black
	310	/ *	403	black
★	666		46	red
○	743		302	yellow
☆	754		1012	peach
▲	797		132	blue
¢	910		229	green

* Use 2 strands of floss.

Design was stitched on an 11" x 10½" piece of White Aida (14 ct) using 3 strands of floss for Cross Stitch and 1 strand for Backstitch except where noted in color key. It was custom framed. Design was also stitched on a prefinished white photo holder (14 ct) using 3 strands of floss for Cross Stitch and 1 strand for Backstitch except where noted in color key.

GENERAL INSTRUCTIONS

łow to Read Charts

ːch chart is made up of a key and a gridded design ʰere each square represents a stitch.
ɔbreviations are used as headings in the key:

X — Cross Stitch
DMC — DMC color numbers
½X — Half Cross Stitch
B'ST — Backstitch
ANC. — Anchor color numbers
Color — the name given to the floss color in this chart

ıe symbols in the key tell you which floss color to
e for each stitch in the chart.

A square filled with a color and a symbol should be worked as a **Cross Stitch** or a **Half Cross Stitch**.

A straight line should be worked as a **Backstitch**.

A large dot listed near the end of the key should be worked as a **French Knot**.

An oval listed near the end of the key should be worked as a **Lazy Daisy Stitch**. The chart will indicate the exact size and placement.

 the chart, when a **Backstitch** crosses a square that s the same color and/or symbol on both sides of e Backstitch, a **Cross Stitch** should be used.

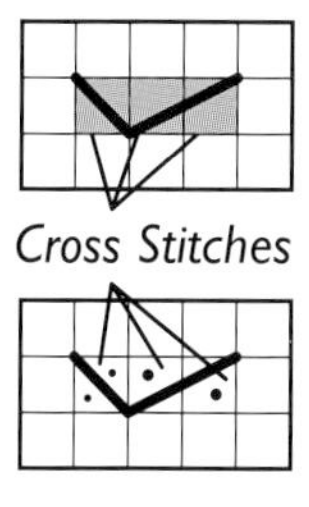

Though not listed separately in the key, a colored triangle ( ) in the chart is usually worked as a **One-Quarter Stitch.** The color of the triangle will match the background color of the corresponding Cross Stitch (or be shown as a smaller dot for the color white).

A colored triangle in the chart should be worked as a **Three-Quarter Stitch** when a Backstitch crosses two squares on the edge of a design,

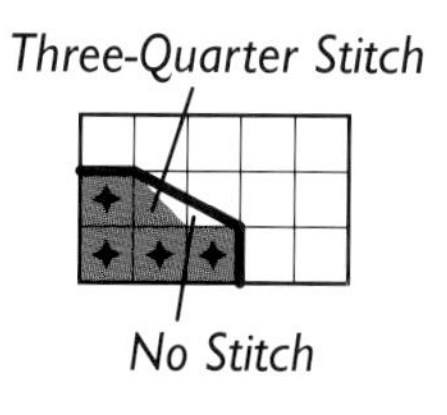

- OR -

when a Backstitch crosses two squares that have white spaces "sandwiched" between two colored triangles.

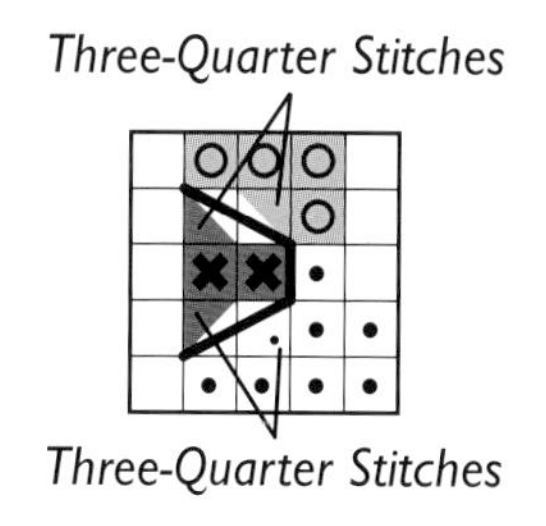

GENERAL INSTRUCTIONS

How to Stitch

Always work **Cross Stitches**, **One-Quarter**, **Half**, and **Three-Quarter Stitches** first and then add the **Backstitch**, **French Knots**, and **Lazy Daisy Stitches**.

Cross Stitch

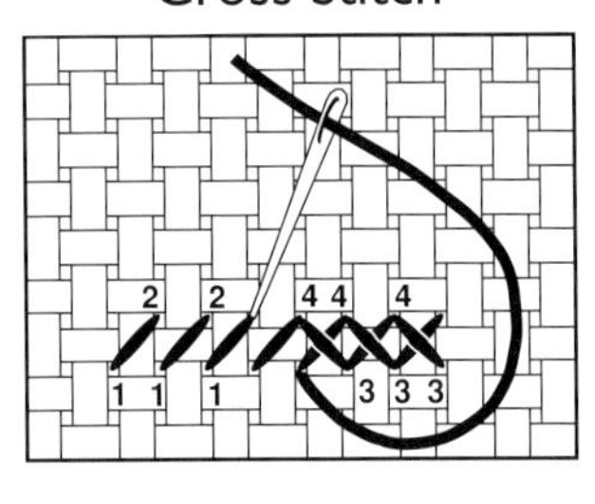

Half Cross Stitch

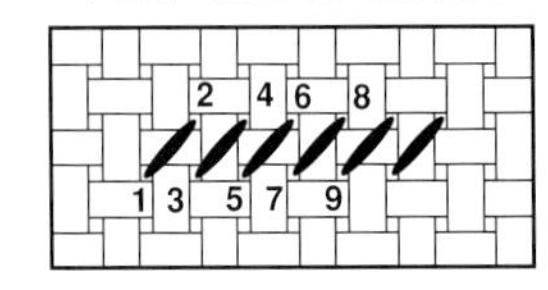

One-Quarter Stitch

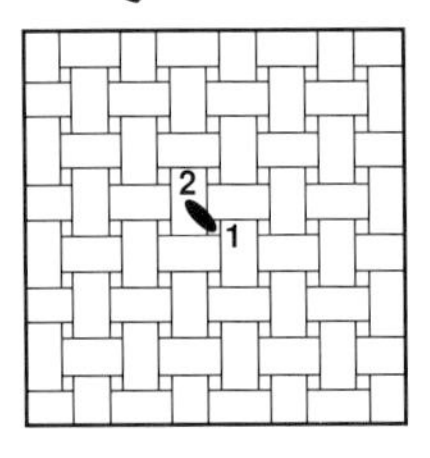

Three-Quarter Stitch

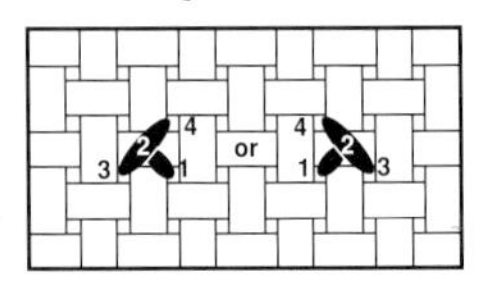

Backstitch

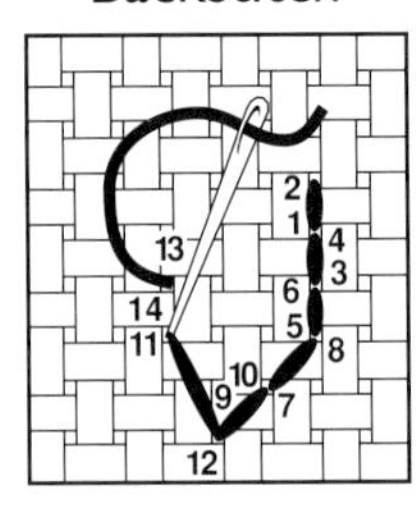

French Knot

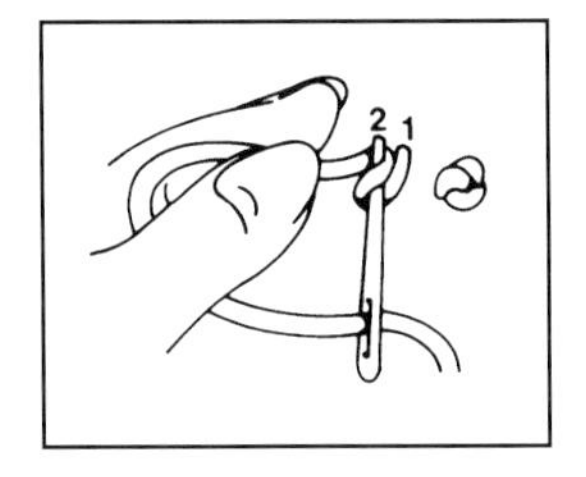

Lazy Daisy Stitch

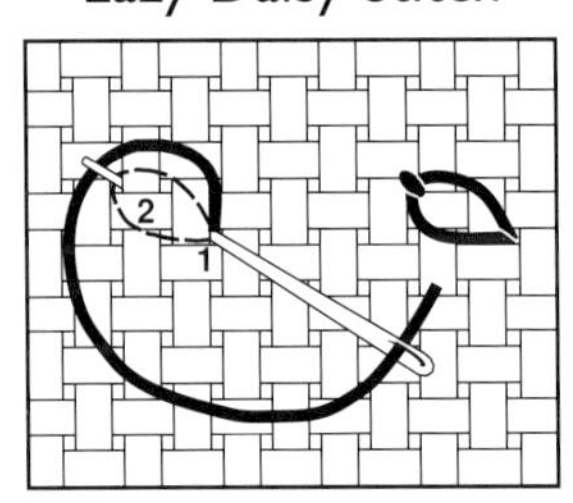

Techniques

Using Waste Canvas

Cut canvas 2" larger than design; baste to garment. To give a firmer stitching base when working on knit fabric, cut a piece of lightweight interfacing 2" larger than hoop and baste to wrong side of fabric. Place garment in hoop; work design using a sharp needle. Trim canvas to within ¾" of design. Dampen canvas slightly to remove sizing. Use tweezers to pull out canvas threads one at a time. Trim interfacing close to design.

Working over Two Fabric Threads

When working over two fabric threads, the stitches should be placed so that vertical fabric threads support each stitch. Make sure that the first Cross Stitch is placed on the fabric with stitch 1-2 beginning and ending where a vertical fabric thread crosses over a horizontal fabric thread.

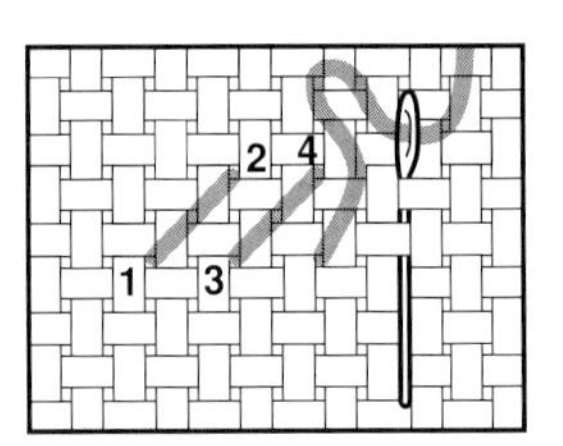